The River Gods
of Greece

THE RIVER GODS OF GREECE

Myths and Mountain Waters in the Hellenic World

HARRY BREWSTER

Preface by Peter Levi

I.B. Tauris Publishers

LONDON · NEW YORK

Published in 1997 by I.B.Tauris & Co Ltd
Victoria House, Bloomsbury Square,
London WC1B 4DZ

Copyright © 1997 by Harry Brewster

A full CIP record for this book is available from the British Library

A full CIP record is available from the Library of Congress

ISBN 1 86064 207 1

Printed and bound in Great Britain by WBC Ltd, Bridgend, Mid
Glamorgan.

Colour origination and printing by Ebenezer Baylis and Son Ltd,
The Trinity Press, Worcester.

To
Meg and James

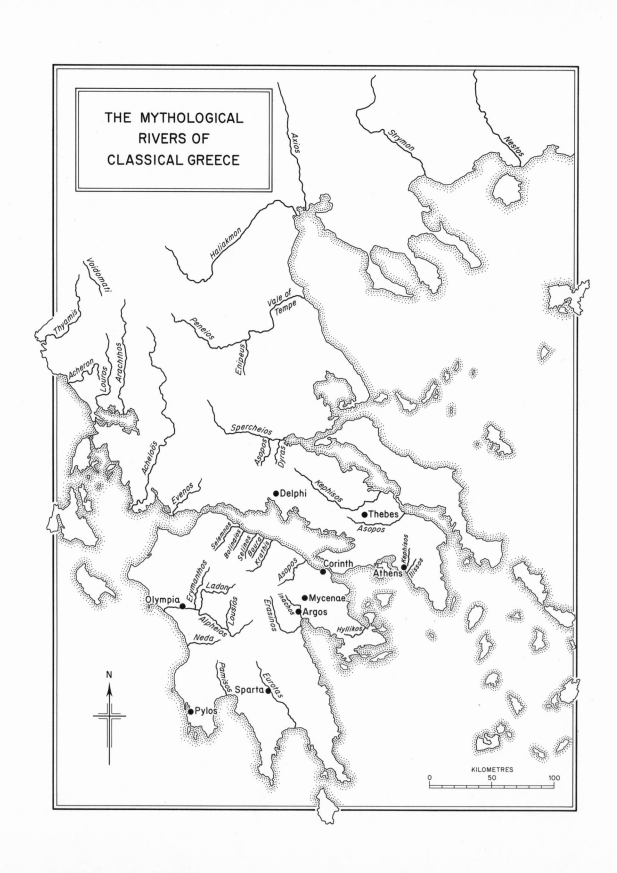

THE MYTHOLOGICAL
RIVERS OF
CLASSICAL GREECE

Axios

Strymon

Nestos

Haliakmon

Voidomati

Vale of
Tempe

Thyamis

Peneios

Acheron

Louros

Arachthos

Enipeus

Achelöis

Spercheios

Asopos

Dyras

Evenos

Kephisos

Delphi

Thebes

Asopos

Selemnos

Bolinaios

Selinos

Boura

Krathis

Kephisos

Erymanthos

Ladon

Asopos

Corinth

Athens

Ilissos

Olympia

Lousios

Inachos

Mycenae

Alpheios

Erasinos

Argos

Neda

Hyllikos

Pamisos

Eurotas

Sparta

Pylos

N

KILOMETRES

0   50   100

CONTENTS

Map: The Mythological Rivers of Classical Greece   vi

Preface by Peter Levi   ix

Introduction   1

PART I **Northwestern Greece**   7

1 The Acheloös: Greece's Great River, Rich in Myths   9

2 The Acheron: River of the Underworld   15

3 The Kokytos: The Other River of the Underworld   20

4 The Evenos: Where Nessos Was Killed   21

5 Other Rivers of Northwestern Greece   27

PART II **Eastern Greece**   31

6 The Peneios and Its Tributaries: Daphne's Father   33

7 The Haliakmon, the Axios, the Strymon and the Nestos   40

8 The Spercheios Loved by Achilles and Its Tributaries   44

9 The Kephisos of Phokis and Boeotia: The Bellowing Bull   47

10 The Boeotian Asopos: A God of Distinguished Progeny   50

11 The Kephisos and Ilissos of Attica   52

PART III **The Peloponnese**   57

12 The Inachos: Punished by Poseidon   59

13 The Erasinos: A Vanished River God   61

14 The Hyllikos and the Golden Stream That Never Dies   63

15 The Selemnos and Other Lesser Streams of the Northern Peloponnese   65

16 The Asopos of Phleius: Sent Home with Thunderbolts   67

17 The Styx: The Terrible Goddess   69

18 The Aroanios and Its Springs: Where the Trout Sang   72

19 The Ladon: Rich in Offspring and in Stories   74

20 The Erymanthos: Haunt of Centaurs   78

21 The Alpheios: A River God Renowned for His Lust   80

22 The Eurotas: Ancestor of Helen   88

23 The Pamisos: A River God of Some Importance   93

24 The Neda and the Lymax: Where Zeus Was Born?   95

    Mythological Rivers and Other Streams of Interest   99
    Notes   101
    Index   110

PREFACE

by Peter Levi

THERE ARE FAR too many books about Greece, but none like this one. It is completely individual, and the outcome of a long, affectionate exploration. As a man, I first knew Harry Brewster as an intrepid traveller and a connoisseur of many neglected corners of the Greek countryside. As a writer, I first encountered him in *Where the Trout Sing*, a splendid and admirably eccentric book I have read many times. His photography is thrilling. It has a dry sparkle and a sense of texture and darkness that transform photography into a fine art. As a medium of illustration for Greece, it can compare with the crisp aquatints and watercolours of a hundred and fifty years ago; it far excels the dull engravings and confused sepia photographs of our grandparents, and the hectic colours of most modern illustrations.

What the text as well as the photography of *The River Gods of Greece* so admirably conveys is the 'quality of water which in motion suggests life'. The text is both highly informative and scholarly, and extremely readable. One begins to see in the mythology as well as the geography of all these rivers that they have distinct personalities and different tones. It is a most original way of introducing a new generation to that combination of secret and unspoilt detail, the exploration of haunted landscapes, and the consideration of ancient literature and ancient beliefs, that taken together are the true basis of Philhellenism.

Some parts of Greece have few rivers, and in this book they hardly figure. Anyone who has seen the huge balloon-like objects, like wasp-coloured icebergs, being towed from island to island in the summer through Greek waters will know what a problem water is in many parts of Greece. But the great rivers have an admirable abundance, and Harry Brewster has made it his mania to explore them all. They are surprisingly numerous. He has also explored adventurously in literature. I am delighted to see he gives credit even to Ovid, who as he remarks is better than Virgil at Greek landscape.

This is not a guidebook or a travel book, or a mythological dictionary. It is a freshly and lucidly written account of a precise and most interesting subject. It is like the conversation of the most interesting possible companion, never too demanding and never boring. It is full of fascinating things one is glad to hear, constantly spirited and reliable. I cannot think of any better introduction to one of the greatest pleasures of life: that of real travelling in attractive and remote places. Those readers past their first youth will extract from it, as one sucks honey out of clover, a literary and vicarious pleasure. For the most fortunate reader, it will let loose a cataract of memory and of fresh curiosity at once. I do not suppose anyone but Harry Brewster has visited all these rivers, and we shall be condemned to envy him until we have equalled him.

It is amazing how important in mythology a stream that seemed obscure or undistinguished can turn out to be. The relation of the river to its own landscape, and the special character it has, are often expressed in ways one had not imagined. One makes the mistake in reading Greek of translating 'river' into a generalized idea. But what could be more individual than the course of rivers? The Alpheios and the splendid Ladon are unlike any other river in Greece. I recommend to any agile reader a pilgrimage to the point where they meet. That is a classic spot, though little visited, but these photographs and this text offer more rarefied adventures.

What gives life in these pages is the vigorous mobility of water, its speed and slowness and its charm in light and shadow, affecting us – as it affects so much of the best Greek landscape – by secrecy and by contrast. Those who visit Greece only in summer have often little idea of the way in which water brings the entire countryside to life. No other European country contains such differences of rainfall in its different regions. To the ancient Greeks the most important voice in their landscape was that of rivers. The fantasies and the hunger and fear that underlie their mythology and so much of their literature linger often on water springs, on streams and on great rivers. Harry Brewster has chosen not only a completely original but also a central subject. This is a book of revelation.

INTRODUCTION

THE LAND OF GREECE is all ruggedness: rock and earth scoured into the bold ribs of an articulate body shaped by millennia of weathering. Its beauty, evoked by poets and described by travellers through the centuries, lies precisely in that wealth and variety its configuration presents where land and sea interlace within a restricted area in a light intensely translucent or delicately hazy according to the season and weather.

The mythology that the ancient people of this country evolved is replete with a unique sense of intimacy as well as familiarity not merely with nature as a whole but with the individual features of the landscape. Famous, for instance, were the mountains, for they stood prominent not only geographically, but also as part and parcel of the mythological world that enveloped the lives of all Hellenes. To all those with some knowledge of Greek mythology the mere mention of the word 'Olympus' stirs up an image of the glorious residence of the gods. Mount Ossa will make them think at once of Pelion being piled upon it by giants in a desperate struggle and Pelion will make them think of Lapiths fighting centaurs eloping with their women. If Parnassus is mentioned perchance they will visualize the Muses conversing in the luminous light of those limestone peaks. If they come across the word 'Helikon' it will conjure up in the mind not only the Muses again but also Bellerophon's horse Pegasos taking off from the summit of the mountain with a kick which opened up a spring, Hippokrene. If you happen to say Mount Kithairon they will see one of those beacons flare up that announced the fall of Troy across the Aegean Sea. You mention Mount Mainalon and they will see Pan roving in its woods. Mount Kyllene will evoke a deep cave in which Hermes was born. And Mount Ida? Well, which Mount Ida do you mean, they will ask, the Cretan Ida connected with the worship of Zeus, or the Ida in Mysia where the judgement of Paris took place and from the summit of which the gods watched the battles on the plain of Troy? And so on. We leap from mountain to mountain with the whole spectrum of mythology from different approaches glittering in Apollonian

1

light or we can roam in the more Dionysian shades of the gorges, their counterpart, along the banks of rivers echoing from the past the songs of the Naiads. For the rivers of Greece are no less evocative. They are, in fact, even closer participants in the life itself of the myths. The mountains formed an important part of the mythological landscape but they remained inanimate, whereas the rivers were characters in the myths, often their protagonists, as well as essential features of the scenery. They were living beings, they were divinities. The mountains, on the other hand, were seldom gods.

There is a quality pertaining to water in motion which suggests life. The myths of ancient Greece show how responsive the people of those days were to the vitality and numinous character of their rivers, or in other words to the mysterious presence of a god which a river would emanate. Both major and lesser poets keep referring to them and bringing them into the landscapes of their most stirring imagery. What is there more suggestive of the numinous life of a river than the picture we are given of the Skamander in the *Iliad*, where the Troad scenery has become part of Greece.

Every spring even, whether gushing or trickling, was mysteriously live, for there was always a nymph presiding or embodying it, not a god but a female deity. As sons of Okeanos and Tethys, rivers were nearly always gods; springs were always female creatures. Their *religio loci* was feminine in contrast to the virile life of rivers.

Every river was numinous though not all played a prominent part in mythology. Some behaved like powerful overlords or active kings, as for instance the Alpheios did, or the Acheloös. Others were more passive and behaved as spectators of the happenings in their waters or on their banks, rather than as direct participants; the Evenus was one of these. Most of them were amorously disposed. They all attended the assemblies of the gods on Mount Olympus,[1] and they received sacrifices from mortals wishing to propitiate them.[2] Many of them had altars erected to them and statues personifying them.[3]

If we glance at the map of continental Greece and look southward from the northern frontiers of Albania and Makedonia to the Gulf of Corinth we at once notice that dividing the country longitudinally is a great chain of mountains, the Pindos, with the regions of Epirus, Akarnania and Aetolia to the west of the range, Makedonia, Thessaly and Boeotia to the east. Nearly all the mythological rivers of northern Greece rise in the Pindos and flow either southwestward into the Ionian Sea or the Gulf of Corinth, like the Acheloös and the Evenos, or eastward into the Aegean sea like the Peneios, the Spercheios, and the Kephisos.

South of the Gulf of Corinth is the Peloponnese rich in important mythological rivers, such as the Alpheios, its tributary the Ladon, the Neda and several others, which flow from the heights of Arcadia northward, westward and southward. The islands, including Crete and Cyprus, have no rivers or streams of any noteworthy mythological interest, except Sicily.

The principal mythological rivers of Greece number about thirty, some of them real rivers flowing with abundant water, others mere streams often shrinking in the summer to a trickle or even drying up altogether, like the Inachos, but mythologically important none the less. All of them reach back into the remote past with surviving numinous elements in their courses that are full of natural beauty. The part they played in the imagination of the people is vividly illustrated in the works of the poets and writers of ancient Greece and Rome.

In addition to the main mythological rivers, about another two dozen are worth taking into account, which strictly speaking are not mythological or did not play as great a part, if any at all, in the myths of Greece. Some flow in outlying areas at the extremities of ancient Hellas, whose local myths for various reasons failed to find their way into literature and become part of the web of Greek mythology such as it was handed down to posterity. Others, even though flowing at the heart of ancient Greece, were evidently eclipsed by more important neighbours. I include several of them in my descriptive survey, however, not only because they are mentioned by Herodotus, Strabo, Pausanias or other writers of the ancient world and because there is often evidence that they were revered as river gods, but above all on account of their natural beauty and that numinous quality they have of which the ancient Greeks were so receptive.

An alphabetical list of the more important rivers, including lesser ones from the point of view of mythology, is appended to the survey.

The natural beauty of all these rivers, which varies a great deal, is determined by certain specific factors and the relation of these to one another: (a) the volume of water they carry, (b) the incline at which they flow and the speed of their current, (c) the character of the scenery in which their courses lie, (d) the vegetation that accompanies them, (e) whether or not they are rocky and full of boulders, (f) the geological nature of these boulders when they constitute a distinctive feature, (g) whether or not they have waterfalls and deep pools. The great rivers in Makedonia and Thrace tend to be dull in spite of their abundance of water and don't reflect very vividly whatever mythological past they have had because of their lethargic flow in flat, open country with few distinctive landmarks. On the other hand even small streams, such as the Hyllikos or the Lymax in the Peloponnese, with relatively little water running in them, can be extremely evocative owing to their remarkable features and the atmosphere they emanate.

Greek mythology is like a wonderful web clinging to the ground and hovering in the air, in contact with the earth and yet suspended above, a gossamer glittering with dewdrops in the sun, for gods and humans would meet here, if not on equal terms behaving alike none the less, in an atmosphere of mutual emotions and deeds. Religion and myth were one, there were no fundamentalists or rationalists trying to tear them apart save a few old, pedantic philosophers. So deeply rooted were the myths in the minds of every man and woman, so familiar with them was everybody in every walk of life, so current were they in people's daily lives, flowing like blood in their veins, that they quite naturally formed the material out of which poets and tragedians, sculptors and painters, created their works. The myths were dealing with life no matter how crowded the scenery was with gods and heroes, nymphs and fanciful creatures. Only later on, in the Hellenistic and Roman world, did the old myths begin to sink away into the background of everyday life (albeit not everywhere), only later on were they manipulated into literary forms, thereby losing much of their vigour.

In this web of myths the great cycles wind round as the main threads that hold the tissue together; all the crisscross offshoots from the same deities and heroes, the lesser myths and the little myths, such as those of Leda, Endymion, Oenome, Hyakinthos, Syrinx, Daphne, and dozens of others, come to complete the intricate and interconnected pattern most wonderfully.

The rivers flow as ever, parts of the pattern, liquid threads numinous and alive, with their legends, their stories, their physical presence ready to be recalled.

The sources I have gone back to in the attempt to rekindle something of their mythological lives are first and foremost Homer and Hesiod, who provide the oldest material on record. Then come the dramatists and other main poets in so far as they touch upon mythological events relating to rivers. Last, but in a way not least, I have had recourse to the mythographers, compilers, late writers and commentators: Apollodoros, Hyginus, Diadorous Siculus, Teztzes, Eustathios and others, including of course the fairly reliable Strabo and the less accurate Pliny the Elder for geographical data and descriptions. The works of mythographers that have survived are relatively late but invaluable nevertheless, because their writers had access to the early mythographers closer to the actual sources of the myths such as Akousilaos, whose works have failed to reach us. Finally Pausanias must be mentioned, that indefatigable traveller and sightseer of the second century AD, for he is a source of the utmost importance from more than one standpoint. He is invaluable not only because of the spontaneous, if somewhat naive, religiosity in his approach to myths relating to the sites he visited and described in the course of his travels, but also because he brings us in touch with the local beliefs still astonishingly alive in his days and full of regional rivalries. I have had recourse to his testimony wherever he touches on rivers. Unfortunately he did not extend his survey into Aetolia and Epirus to the northwest and into the regions north of Boeotia on the east of the Pindos where several important rivers flow.

I have found Apollodoros most useful in spite of his much-disparaged uncritical hotchpotch of approach. Inasmuch as he is a naive mythographer he is far more reliable than the late poets who used and manipulated mythology for literary purposes. Virgil provides examples of the abuse that can be made of mythology by dragging in and mixing mythological elements that have nothing to do with each other in order to achieve certain literary effects. But from time to time I do quote from Ovid at length because of the vivacity of his imagery, though he too is guilty of some mixing. This poet, who was to be the main channel through which myths came down to us before other sources were little by little made available, is more reliable than Virgil, having no political or extraneous motives in his *Metamorphoses* for excessive distortion or arbitrary modification. His poetic fantasy did not lead him beyond reasonable limits as Virgil was led in dealing, for instance, with the myth of Aristaios.[4] Ovid is a great embroiderer, of course, but the skein from which he draws the threads of his embroidery is sound and remains sound. His descriptive imagination helps one to conjure up the whole picture of a mythological event.

The elaborateness of the web would be far greater if so many pertinent records had not been lost in the course of time, but what has survived is rich enough for us to call up something of the numinous wonder of these rivers, with which we can come in touch through our senses as well as our minds.

The nineteenth century was the century of the rediscovery of Greece, the century of travellers, not tourists, who set out to find whatever had survived of Hellas. They were mainly topographers and skilful sketchers, interested in the geography as well as in the ancient sites of the country which had ceased to be surveyed since the days of Strabo and Pausanias: men such as Edward Dodwell, William Gell, Thomas Hughes, Henry Holland, John Hawkins, François Pouqueville and Edward Lear. Supreme amongst them was William Leake, the Pausanias of the early nineteenth century, less religiously minded than he, but no less pedestrian and devoted to the task of observing and recording. The nineteenth-century travellers were men equipped with a good knowledge of the ancient world, of the Greek language and Greek literature, such as every gentleman possessed in those days. Most of them, however, were strictly speaking not scholars, and so it is perhaps not surprising that the rivers are mentioned by them as part of the geography of the country, but hardly at all, except in the case of some famous watercourses like Tempe, as part of the historical and cultural setting of ancient Greece. Though responsive to the quality of the scenery and to the picturesque, they were primarily interested in ruins. More surprising is that the mythological nature and cultural implications of these rivers, which were the river gods of old, should have been overlooked in the twentieth century, the century of academics, tourists and guidebooks.

The object of this book is not that of a guidebook, nor that of a travel book, of which there are already far too many.

By describing and photographing the rivers of Greece such as they are today and by recalling what the poets, mythographers and historians have said about them, I have set out to conjure up from the past, as far as possible, the mythological landscape in which these rivers were felt to be deities and revered as such.[5]

I

NORTHWESTERN GREECE

THE WHOLE OF northwestern Greece – Epirus, Akarnania and Aitolia – is dominated by two elements of its geological formation, two types of rock, which confer upon the scenery its distinctive character. These are flysch and limestone. Flysch is the geological term for a rock consisting of sequences of shale interbedded with sandstone, marls, clay and conglomerate. It is a rock of somewhat crumbly consistency and indeterminate colour ranging from brown to shades of grey.

Regions of limestone and flysch alternate from the Ionian Sea border eastward to the Pindos range and beyond. Where limestone prevails the ground rises in majestic shapes with lofty mountain peaks, usually bare and of a luminous colour varying from white to pink, ochre and light grey. The vegetation, mainly kermes oak, clings to the ground and manages to grow, but only where the high degree of drainage characteristic of this terrain permits some moisture to collect and where erosion has not set in as a result of unrestrained nibbling by the ubiquitous goat. In the river beds, boulders and pebbles accumulate washed down, rounded and smoothed by torrential currents, shining brilliantly white in the sun.

Where flysch prevails the configuration is softer and usually covered in vegetation. The ground is only partly cultivated. As well as maquis, trees are not lacking, mainly oak, pine, elm, plane and poplar, standing alone or in groves, or even forming forests as in the Zagoria region. Although the ground, when laid bare, is not as attractive as in the limestone areas, the landscape does not necessarily lack beauty because the configuration is nearly always articulate, often with bold limestone eminences on the horizon.

A certain amount of alluvial soil is to be found in the lower regions, but only where the rivers, as they approach the sea, flow on virtually level ground.

Epirus, or strictly speaking Epeirus – 'the continent' as the term itself says – with its Tymphe and Pindos limestone peaks covered in snow for most of the year round and with its other cloud-gathering mountains such as Tomaros overlooking Dodona, is of the three northwestern regions of Greece by far the richest in rivers, streams and springs. These many rivers and streams are fed by the winter snows and rains that prevail at those altitudes.

Akarnania, immediately to the south of Epirus, is conspicuously lacking in rivers and streams of any size or mythological significance. It has, however, a couple of pleasant lakes. The border between Akarnania and Aitolia is formed by the river Acheloös which rises in the Pindos heights to the north, between Epirus and Thessaly. It is the largest river in Greece, a river god of outstanding mythological importance.

There are a few more lakes in Aitolia, but rivers are scarce there as well. However, the only one of any size, the Evenos, is of fascinating mythological interest.

1

THE ACHELOÖS

Greece's Great River, Rich in Myths

FAIR-FLOWING ACHELOÖS, river god and king of all the rivers in Greece, the biggest and fullest, father of the Sirens, the oldest and most revered of the three thousand streams to which Okeanos and Tethys gave birth. The horn of plenty.

Its waters were silvery, so Hesiod tells us to denote their rippling clarity.[1] Indeed Acheloös was river god and king, as the ancient poets of Greece and Rome from Homer through the centuries regarded him. And kingly the river still is today in its natural and evocative beauty, albeit a small stream compared with the great rivers of the world.

Achilles, exulting in his victory over his opponent Asteropaios who boasted of being the son of the mighty river Axios, exclaims that no river can vie with him Achilles, a descendant of Zeus, not even King Acheloös.[2]

Acheloös was not only father of the Sirens[3] but also of the nymphs who would 'range swiftly in the dance about him',[4] and of many a spring. So for instance, a spring nymph of Aitolia, who married the hero Alkmaion, was a daughter of Acheloös;[5] and so was the famous spring Kastalia of Delphi,[6] sacred to the Muses. Euripides as a matter of course refers to the 'holy spring of Dirke', in which Dionysus had bathed, as Acheloös' daughter.[7] Nor could the lyric poets refrain from responding to the imagery of the river's beauty, with a gentler-than-usual picture such as Pindar conjures up when he says about the syrinx, 'Thou, the most musical reed, was once nurtured by the spring of fair-flowing Acheloüs.'[8]

An extremely live, personified picture of the river both as god and wooer is given to us by Sophocles in his *Trachiniae* through the main female character of the tragedy, Deianeira, King Oeneos's daughter. She tells the audience:

I, who in the house of my father Oeneus, while yet I dwelt in Pleuron, had such fear of marriage as never vexed any maiden in Aetolia. For my wooer was a river god, Acheloüs, who in three shapes was ever asking me from my father, coming now as a bull in bodily form, now as a serpent with sheeny coils, now with a trunk of man and a front of ox, while from a shaggy beard the streams of fountain-water flowed abroad.[9]

Later, the chorus gives an account of the wrestling contest between Acheloös and Herakles as suitors of Deianeira:

One was a mighty river god, the dread form of a horned and four-legged bull, Acheloös, from Oeniadai; the other came from Thebe, dear to Bakchos, with curved bow, and spears, and brandished club, the son of Zeus; who met in combat, fain to win a bride: and the Cyprian goddess of nuptial joy was there with them, sole umpire of the strife. Then was there clatter of fists and clang of bow, and the noise of a bull's horns therewith; then were there close-locked grapplings, and deadly blows from the forehead, and loud deep cries from both. Meanwhile she, in her delicate beauty, sat on the side of a hill that could be seen afar, awaiting the husband that should be hers.[10]

The protean quality of the river god stirred the imagination of Ovid who found in the events referred to by Sophocles ideal material for his theme in the *Metamorphoses*. Indeed he revels in the story, and the picture he gives us is delightfully florid. Acheloös receives Theseus, who is on his way back to Athens after having taken part in the Calydonian boar hunt, and tells him about his fight with Herakles with whom he disputed the hand of Deianeira. He says that on the verge of being beaten he had recourse to stratagems before giving in:

['I] slipped from the hero's grasp by turning myself into a long snake. But when I had coiled my body into sinuous spirals, and was flickering my forked tongue, hissing fiercely, Hercules of Tiryns laughed, and mocked my tricks. "I was defeating snakes in my cradle!" he cried, "and though you may be more terrible than any other, Acheloüs, yet you are only one solitary serpent, and how small a part of the Lernaean hydra that will be! The hydra throve on its wounds, and none of its hundred heads could be cut off with impunity, without being replaced by two new ones which made its neck stronger than ever. Yet, in spite of its branching snakes, reborn as they were cut down, in spite of the strength it derived from attempts to harm it, still I got the upper hand of the hydra, vanquished the monster, and ripped its body open. Imagine, then, what will happen to you, who have changed yourself into a mere semblance of a snake, employing weapons that are not natural to you, and concealing yourself under a borrowed shape!" With these words, he fastened his fingers tightly round the upper part of my throat. I was being throttled, as if my neck were caught in a vice, and struggled to wrest my jaws out of the grip of his thumbs.

10

'So he overcame me in this guise too; but there remained my third shape, that of a fierce bull. I therefore transformed myself into a bull, and as such renewed the fight. My adversary, attacking me from the left, flung his arms round the bulging muscles of my neck. As I charged away, he followed close behind me, dragging at my head, till he forced my horns into the hard ground, and laid me prostrate in the deep dust. Nor was this enough: as he grasped my stiff horn in his cruel hand, he broke and tore it off, mutilating my brow. But the naiads filled it with fruits and fragrant flowers, and sanctified it, and now my horn enriches the Goddess of Plenty.'[11] (Plate 5)

Ovid adds that when Acheloös had finished speaking, one of his attendants, a nymph dressed in the style of Artemis, came forward, her hair streaming over her shoulders, and brought all sorts of fruit in the horn for their dessert.

So the cornucopia, prominent through the ages as a symbol of plenty, came into being from the broken-off horn of Acheloös, the river being a source of fertility and hence of plenty (Plates 6 and 7).[12] Ovid goes on to say:

> However, the loss of this adornment, taken from him by Hercules, was the only humili-
> ation Acheloüs suffered: in all other respects he was unhurt, and he concealed his loss
> by wearing on his head a wreath of willow leaves, or of reeds.

A Roman poet, Ovid of course wrote many centuries after the Greek myths had come into being. In his *Metamorphoses* he included stories some of which were very ancient and others of relatively recent vintage. Though neither Homer nor Hesiod say anything about this wrestling contest, it is without any doubt a very old myth. Long before Sophocles' account we find, on a sixth-century BC Attic vase, the story of the struggle and the river god's transformation most vividly depicted by Oltos, one of the prominent vase painters of those days. We see Acheloös changing from snake into bull and Herakles grasping one of his horns (Plate 5).

Theseus' visit had put Acheloös in an excellent mood, so Ovid tells us. The distinguised guest was so heartily welcomed that barefooted nymphs at once set out tables and loaded them with good things to eat, no doubt from the cornucopia. The river god gave Theseus a poetic account of how the Echinades islands had come into existence, the hero having pointed them out on the horizon. They were not islands once upon a time, Acheloös explained, but nymphs who misbehaved by omitting to invite him to a banquet they were giving, and so in a fit of vexation he flooded them and turned them into islands off the coast. This of course happened in mythical days. By the time historians and geographers started writing, some had already been silted up; evidently the river's punishment had not stopped at the nymphs being transformed into islands. Herodotus says:

> I could mention other rivers also, far inferior to the Nile in magnitude, that have effected
> very great changes. Among these not the least is the Acheloüs which, after passing
> through Acarnania, empties itself into the sea opposite the islands called Echinades and
> has already joined one half of them to the continent.[13]

11

This process of the alluvial plain extending into the sea and joining up with the islands interested not only Herodotus but also Thucydides who devoted a whole passage to it in his *History of the Peloponnesian War*:

> The river Acheloüs flowing from Mount Pindus through Dolopia and the country of the Agraeans and Amphilochians and the plain of Acarnania, past the town of Stratus in the upper part of its course, forms lakes where it falls into the sea round Oeniadae, and thus makes it impracticable for any army in winter by reason of the water. Opposite to Oeniadae lie most of the islands called Echinades, so close to the mouths of the Acheloüs that the powerful stream is constantly forming deposits against them, and has already joined some of the islands to the continent, and seems likely in no long while to do the same to the rest. For the current is strong, deep and turbid, and the islands are so thick together that they serve to imprison the alluvial deposit and prevent its dispersing, lying, as they do, not in one line, but irregularly, so as to leave no direct passage for the water into the open sea. The islands in question are uninhabited and of no great size.[14]

A few centuries later Strabo, in describing the geographical layout of the river between Akarnania and Aitolia, proceeds to demythologize in his typical matter-of-fact manner:

> It was this silt which in earlier times caused the country called Paracheloitis, which the river overflows, to be a subject of dispute between the Acarnanians and Aetolians; for they would decide the dispute by arms, since they had no arbitration, and the more powerful of the two would win the victory; and this is cause of the fabrication of a certain myth, telling how Heracles defeated Acheloüs and as the prize of his victory won the hand of Deianeira, the daughter of Oeneus.[15]

Demythologizing has gone on of course. The river god's forces have been harnessed for irrigation and power generation. His impetuous waters are nowadays controlled by a great dam constructed some years ago and by the creation of a large artificial lake halfway down the river's course with hydroelectric power installations. The economic reasons may be most valid, but from my point of view I hold no brief for such major alterations to the configuration of the land, for the natural course of the river being interrupted and transformed. Moreover there always is, to my mind, something uncanny and unpleasant about an artificial lake. Along most of its course, however, the Acheloös has retained much of its personality, its mystery, its gripping character.

Through Pindos's glens and gorges the river rushes southward from its source high up in the mountains (Plate 1), shaping rock and boulder into sculpture, smoothing the stones and pebbles into globes that glisten like marble in the sun or moon, roaring, gurgling, purling waters that keep licking the gnarled roots that emerge from under plane trees and willows. Tributaries from the melting snows of ranges on either side of its course pour in, eager to augment its volume.

Aspropotamos, meaning 'the white river', is the name by which the Acheloös has been known for some time. In fact its waters are blue and green, rather than white, but in modern Greek *aspros* can also mean clear and pure; and indeed so unpolluted is the river in its upper reaches that the water is delicious to drink as well as to swim in (Plate 1).

The source of the Acheloös is to be found in the upper folds of Mount Lakmon, the Peristeri of our times – Aspripigi (Ἄσπρη Πηγή), as the shepherds call the spring presumably because it pours over a white rock, perhaps one of the reasons why the Acheloös has been called the Aspropotamos. Only recently has it been given its ancient name again.

Away to the southeast is a tributary, the present-day Tauropos, known locally as the Migdovas, which was regarded by Thucydides[16] and Strabo[17] as the upper course of the Acheloös. The main branch was referred to as the Inachos.[18] Strabo, however, had evidently not visited the region since he contradicted himself saying elsewhere that the Inachos flowed into the Ambrakian gulf.[19] In fact he based his account of the Inachos as tributary of the Acheloös on what he says Sophocles had stated. The Tauropos, or Migdovas, rises in the mountain of Dolopia, near the present town of Karditsa, where an artificial lake has been made at its source, and then joins the Aspropotamos in Aitolia. But this branch of the river is a much shorter and lesser stream, so one is fully warranted to regard the Aspropotamos as the real upper course of the Acheloös.

The uppermost reaches of the Acheloös consist of a little stream which flows through flysch country, where the Pindos range is not as spectacular as on its western side in Epirus. The geological formation of the region is tame by comparison, green, pastoral, with gentle declivities suitable for flocks of sheep which abound. But the spring itself is worthy of the great river, pouring over a huge rock on boulders enshrined in thick vegetation.

There is something wonderful about a spring where a river is born, where the beginning goes on being the beginning century after century, indeed no less wonderful than the mouth of a river with its persistent mingling kiss to the sea, the end that continues to be the end. A spring was always female, always a nymph that gave birth to the river god, for contact between water and earth, or the welling up of water from the earth, had the life-giving nature of the womb.

About ten miles downstream from its source, after having been fed by several springs along its banks and some tributaries, the Acheloös assumes in narrower defiles, under the limestone Zoumerka pinnacles, the grandeur of a mountain river. It is here, in these upper reaches toilsome to get at, in the deep blue pools between boulders and waterfalls, and among the plane trees on its banks, under beetling cliffs and towering crags, that the numinous nature of the river survives as yet undisturbed. The river god and the Naiads are still alive. And it is here that one is tempted to conjure up the figure of Alkmaion who came to be purified by the river god from the taint of having murdered his mother.[20]

Further down the stream, below the dam and the still waters of the artificial lake, the Acheloös resumes its headlong course fed by tributaries, deep, broad and remarkably blue, a river worthy of its mytholopoeic history (Plate 2). As the valley opens out among lower hills, the banks become thickly covered with willows, eucalyptus, brushwood, oleander and reeds; but on either side, beyond this strip of jungly vegetation, are intensely cultivated fields benefiting from irrigation. From the ancient walls of Stratos you get an impressive view of the great mass of water pouring over a dam under the highway bridge.

In the Aitolian plain the river slows down, but flows still plentifully and scarcely muddy in spite of its burden of silt, as it winds its way southwestward to the sea through cultivated fields and marshes. The Echinades islands loom on the horizon, those mischievous nymphs turned into stone and earth for their lapse in etiquette, some already part of the mainland, hills rising abruptly from the smooth, flat surrounding land.

On one of these isolated prominences are situated the ruins of Oeniadai, one of the most enchanting sites of Greece, as yet unspoilt by mass tourism and the administrative measures that inevitably follow. It was founded in mythological times by the hero Alkmaion who, guilty of matricide, had come to King Acheloös for purification. The river god not only purified him of his crime but gave him also his daughter Kallirhoe, a spring nymph, in marriage. Alkmaion settled on the land formed by the alluvial deposits of the river, rich in vines as the name Oeniadai suggests. It grew into a prosperous city with a busy harbour, of which the layout, cut into the hillside, is still conspicuous today. Looking down from the walls, city gates and towers that rise among the oak trees, you see the marshy plain formed by the Acheloös stretching out on all sides with the Echinades islands enlivening the horizon.

As the Acheloös advances towards the sea in winding loops, it broadens but remains deep and remarkably blue with reeds along its banks which are now and then shaded by poplars and willows. Little by little the sea comes nearer. The former Echinades island of Koutailares rears itself sheer from the flat alluvial plain which has reached out gripping it without yet encircling it. Finally there is a lagoon. Aquatic birds swarm over the bulrushes in the stillness of enclosed waters. But the Acheloös, within well-defined banks, advances further and further, its mouth widening for the kiss of the tideless sea and the unburdening of its whole body. The blue-green of its sweet water mingles with the opalescent blue of the salt sea under the rays of the relentless sun. The banks sink away, the reeds disappear, herons and egrets swarm over the lagoon to mix with gulls which come whirling and screaming from over the waves. *Thalassa*, *thalassa*. The great width of the horizon stretches out into a single line broken only by the jagged cliffs of one isle. There, right in front of the river's open mouth, surges Oxeia, a real island, defying the wrath of King Acheloös (Plate 4).

1 The Acheloös, here near its source in the Pindos mountains, was the oldest river god and regarded by the ancient poets of Greece and Rome, from Homer to Ovid, as the most revered of all the rivers in Greece.

2 The Acheloös, in mid-stream flowing abundantly after the contribution of its tributaries, stirred the imagination of Sophocles and Ovid who, because of its powerful flow, endowed the river god with protean qualities, not least those of a powerful suitor.

3 An Etruscan bronze mask of Acheloös depicts the river god in human form, with shaggy beard and horned head, as described by Sophocles in his play *Trachiniae*. (© National Museum of Denmark)

4 The island of Oxeia surges from the sea facing the mouth of the Acheloös as if to defy the king of the river gods' rush into the Ionian Sea.

5 Acheloös, here depicted on a Greek amphora of the sixth century BC in combat with Herakles over the hand of the princess Deianeira, transformed himself from a serpent to a bull, whose horn Herakles was able to grasp and tear off.

6 (above) The Nile, in this Hellenistic interpretation as a river god, reclines on a cornucopia from which pours forth symbols of Egypt's plenty, demonstrating Herodotus' observation, 'Egypt is the gift of the Nile'.

7 (left) The cornucopia, here held by one of Gianbologna's figures in the Renaissance period Ammanati fountain in Florence, traced its origins to the horn of Acheloös, which after being torn off by Herakles was, according to Ovid, immediately filled by naiads with 'fruits and fragrant flowers'. Thus from the myth of Acheloös the cornucopia through the ages has come to symbolise fertility and plenty.

8 The Acheron's natural beauty belies the sinister image attributed to it by mythology and literature as the fearful god and father of a daemon of Hades.

9 The Acheron, fearful river of the Underworld, rises in Thesprotia in northwestern Greece. Described in awed terms by Homer and Plato, it was the river the departing souls had to cross to reach their final destination in Hades.

10 The Acheron, here shown not far from its outlet into the Ionian Sea, flows past a green and tranquil plain which was once the dreaded swampy lake of the Underworld, Palus Acherusia.

CHAPTER

2

THE ACHERON
River of the Underworld

MYSTERIOUS ACHERON! Throughout Greek literature referred to many a time, mentioned by name and invoked with awe, in mythology prominent amongst rivers, yet scarcely a personal deity to whom worship was offered, too fearful, perhaps, as the river of the underworld beyond which there was no return (Plate 8). But a river god he was none the less, married to Gorgyra and father of Askalaphos, a daemon of Hades.[1]

Homer, who places the watercourse in the mythical land of the Cimmerians,[2] allows its geography to remain vague, but its location in Thesprotia was soon established, and it has remained there ever since. The tall poplars and willows[3] of Persephone's grove under the walls of the Nekyomanteion, the Oracle of the Dead, are still to be seen on the banks of the river.

Herodotus says that Periander, the seventh-century BC tyrant of Corinth, sent a messenger to consult the oracle 'concerning a pledge which had been given in his charge by a stranger'.[4]

Charon, son of Erebos, was very busy there, rowing the departed souls across the river. Thus Alkestis, who died for the sake of her husband, was taken away:

> O Daugther of Pelias,
> Hail to you in the house of Hades.
> In the sunless home where you shall dwell!
> Let Hades, the dark-haired God,
> Let the old man, Leader of the Dead,
> Who sits at the oar and helm,

15

> Know you:
> Far, far off is the best of women
> Borne beyond the flood of Acheron
> In the two-oared boat![5]

The white poplar, which grew on the banks of the Acheron's lower course as it flowed into the awesome swamp of the underworld, Palus Acherusia, was famous for having been introduced into Greece from this region by Herakles. Pausanias[6] tells us:

> The Eleans are wont to use for their sacrifices to Zeus the wood of the white poplar and of no other tree, preferring the white poplar simply and solely because Herakles brought it into Greece from Thesprotia. ... Herakles found the white poplar growing on the banks of the Acheron, the river in Thesprotia, and for this reason Homer calls it Acheroid.[7]

According to Apollodoros, Herakles marched with the Calydonians against the Thesprotians. 'Having taken the city of Ephyra, of which Phylas was king, he had a love affair with the king's daughter Astyoche and became the father of Tlepolemus.'[8]

The Dark Lake, as Sophocles calls the swamp,[9] which formed a gulf or lagoon by the sea, was sweetened by the waters of the river and its tributaries.[10] On a prominence overlooking the swamp stood Ephyra which was visited not only by Herakles but also by Odysseos (if credence is to be given to Pallas Athena),[11] and likewise by Theseus who invaded Thesprotia to carry off the wife of the Thesprotian king. No wonder he got into serious difficulties, for he was taken prisoner by the king and held in captivity for a while.[12]

In the minds of Greek poets and writers generally, the awesome image of the Acheron kept fluctuating from a position of sheer myth and fantasy to a more historical and geographically concrete stance. Plato gives us a picture that is terrifyingly fantastic. Flowing in a contrary direction to the Ocean, which is conceived of as a vast stream circulating round the world, the Acheron passes through desert places and under the surface of the earth.

> It reaches the Acherusian lake, where the souls of most who die arrive, and having remained there for certain destined periods, some longer, some shorter, are again sent forth in the generations of animals. A third river issues midway between these [the Ocean and the Acheron], and near its source falls into a vast region, burning with abundance of fire, and forms a lake larger than the sea, boiling with water and mud; from hence it proceeds in a circle, turbulent and muddy, and folding itself round reaches both the places and the extremity of the Acherusian lake, but does not mingle with its water, but folding itself many a time beneath the earth it discharges itself into the lower parts of the Tartarus. And this is the river they call Periphlegeton, whose burning streams emit dissevered fragments in whatever part of the earth they happen to be.[13]

With no less flamboyant strokes of fantasy Plato goes on to describe the Styx and the

Kokytos as part of a whole region on the threshold of Tartaros. This terrifying picture is picked up again by Virgil and handed down to Dante. Virgil, of course, for patriotic reasons, places the region right away from Thesprotia, in Italy, between Cumae and Puteoli – the Avernus Lacus.[14] Taking a more realistic approach, Thucydides gives a succinct geographical description:

Sailing from Leucas the Corinthians made land at a part of the continent opposite Corcyra. They anchored in the harbour of Chimerium, in the territory of Thesprotia, above which, at some distance from the sea, lies the city of Ephyra, in the Elean district. By this city the Acherusian lake pours its waters into the sea. It gets its name from the river Acheron, which flows through Thesprotia and falls into the lake.[15]

Nowadays the lake has become a somewhat marshy plain, partly cultivated. The whole layout of the river through its gorge into the flat, swampy lower reaches as far as the sea, can be encompassed by the eye from the Souli fortresses built by Ali Pasha at the beginning of the nineteenth century on the overlooking mountain crags. The site is memorable for the struggle for freedom and independence by the Christian Albanians, who dwelt in these mountains, from the rule of the terrible tyrant of Epirus. So it has become a place of pilgrimage for patriotic Greeks and has been made easily accessible by a fairly good, though circuitous, road from Glyky built in recent years. Consequently the beautiful Acheron gorge, through which the old way led up to Souli, has been left virtually untouched and unscarred. The most arousing description I have come across of the view from the high-perched fortresses is to be found in the account of Henry Holland who travelled there in 1812:

The Seraglio of Souli is included within the area of the great fortress, recently erected by Ali Pasha. In architecture it is much the same as other Turkish buildings; in situation it is scarcely perhaps to be paralleled. From the great gallery you look down a precipice not much less, probably, than a thousand feet in height, into the dark waters of the river below, which so seen, is a fair representative of the ancient Acheron. On every side is the scenery of the wildest and most extraordinary nature, with disorderly magnificence about it, which forms perhaps its most striking peculiarity. The mountains and the precipices, all on the greatest scale, are thrown confusedly around, as if some other agency than the slow working of nature had operated to produce these effects. The eye, looking generally over the scene, is perplexed at first by its vastness and intricacy, and requires some time to select the objects on which to repose. Towards the south, and over the peaked summits which environ the Seraglio, is seen the long chasm-like channel of the Acheron, beyond it the country stretching down to the gulf of Arta, the gulf itself and the mountains of Acarnania in the remote distance. To the west, you look down precipices intersected by deep ravines to that point of the river, where, receiving the stream of Zagouri from the north, it turns at once to the west, continuing its course from its confined channel to the wide and fertile plains of Paramythia. Its windings on the plains may be far traced, while the distant landscape embraces the sea and chains of hills stretching along the coast.[16]

17

In the southwestern part of the Acherusian marsh a few hills rise here and there, conelike in shape, which look like little islands. No doubt they once were islands, in those distant days when the sea swept in, forming a gulf which only little by little became a lagoon and then a swamp. On one of these stood the Thesprotian city of Ephyra, a settlement dating back to Mycenean times, where Herakles had, as usual, a love affair with the local princess. The city's scattered remains are still to be found on top of the hill.

A few miles further west, overlooking the confluence of the Acheron and the Kokytos, rises another hill, crowned with some fine polygonal walls and other ancient remains. Here stood the Nekyomanteion, Persephone's sanctuary, most appropriately and beautifully situated. Another few miles westward and the Acheron reaches the sea. Until a few years ago this spot was one of the most bewitching sites in Greece, so solitary, so hauntingly sequestered and peaceful. Indeed full of desolate beauty was the atmosphere that hovered around, clinging like mist to the ground, to the Acherusian waters which flowed out into the sea, to the rounded limbs of sand lapped by the waves. Indeed, tethered to the closer bank of the river, as the traveller came to it under swaying willows, there was always an empty boat with oars ready for him or her to be rowed across into a swampy desolation that kept shimmering further and further away, where the flutter of a wing or the mournful cry of a white egret might yet arouse his or her languishing senses. Death would be on the lips of the traveller. Now the place has been commercialized. There are hotels and Coca-Cola. Pop music blares. One does not talk about death. But Charon's boat is still there.

The most impressive stretch of the Acheron's course, however, is not the green and now happy-looking plain, the once-dreaded Palus Acherusia, through which the river flows before emptying itself into the sea, but the deep gorge itself in which it runs as far as Glyki, the ancient site of Glykys, on the edge of the former swamp, now only slightly marshy. Away inland, the Acheron rises in the Thesprotian mountains east of the Souli range and flows for several miles a tame trickle of a stream, until it receives an impetuous tributary in a wooded glen right under the sight of the fortresses that tower a thousand feet above. Here, enriched with this supply of water, the Acheron suddenly gathers momentum and with roaring force forges down the famous gorge which is only a few miles in length, but of imposing grandeur.

There has been a tendency on the part of travellers, especially of the nineteenth century, influenced no doubt by the river's image in literature and mythology, to see gloom as well as grandeur in this cleft through which the frightful stream flowed under crags dripping with blood.[17]

Far from sinister I have always found this gorge, which I have visited many a time, a little paradise of natural beauty, a happy Garden of Eden practically untouched by the outside world. A passage through a tunnel in the cliff has now obviated the need to negotiate the path on the 'perilous ledge along the side of the mountain', as Leake described it and such as I experienced it on my first visit in the 1960s. But the bottom of the gorge at its most beautiful spot, where the verdant valley narrows into a defile of sheer rock, is still only accessible on foot or on a mule by a rough, stony and steep trail only used by charcoal-burners.[18] As you descend to the stream through a forest of ilex trees, with the Souli fortresses looming high above on the other side, the roar of rushing water comes closer. Suddenly, under cliffs bedecked with moss, festooned with ivy and shaded by outstretching holm oak, you catch sight of a luminous mass of contorted white rocks through which the stream hurtles with boisterous impetuosity. These are not boulders as in the upper reaches of the Acheloös or the Arachthos, but part of the river banks themselves, the limestone on either side having been laid bare and carved into fantastic shapes of great beauty by the force of the current (Plates 9 and 10).

This is scenery where the close-up features and details dominate, like that of many mountain streams in Greece, which in the nature of things is seldom panoramic. Grandeur, however, is by no means precluded. Here where we stand on the banks of the fateful Acheron, the sweeping declivities of the valley thickly wooded, the beetling mountain crests, the steep cliffs of the gorge verging on the perpendicular and about to close in upon the stream, are indeed awe-inspiring. But the immediate situation is bewitching, the foreground close around and at our feet where the ground is of a stone that has been turned into sculpture by the hand of nature (Plate 8). The symphony of colours and every detail – the moss, the lichens, the myrtle in bloom, the overhanging branches of plane and ilex, the butterflies and tortoises, the waterfalls and green pools in basins of white limestone shaped and smoothed by the water, spangling shoals of fish in ripples widening under the shining lip of a rock – all converge here, delighting in the harmony of the whole.

This is indeed one of the most enchanting spots of Greece, where any departed soul could be happy to dwell, or at least tarry, before moving on to wherever it is destined to go.

THE KOKYTOS

The Other River of
the Underworld

As ONE OF the four rivers of Hades, the Kocytos holds a respectable place in mythology by the side of the Acheron, into which it flows. Already Homer mentions it. In giving instructions to Odysseos on how to descend into the underworld, Circe says:

> When in thy ship thou hast now crossed the stream of Oceanus, where is a level shore and the groves of Persephone – tall poplars, and willows that shed their fruit – there do thou beach thy ship by the deep eddying Oceanus, but go thyself to the dark House of Hades. There into the Acheron flow Pyriphlegeton and Cocytus, which is a branch of the water Styx; and there is a rock, and the meeting place of the two roaring rivers.[1]

There is no rock, and far from roaring or being terrifying as Plato describes it,[2] the Kokytos is in actual fact a very tame, insignificant stream of no outstanding beauty, though neither is it 'highly unpleasant' as Pausanias would have it.[3]

The Pyriphlegeton, if at all geographically identifiable, is a miserable little stream nowadays. The Styx finds itself in the Peloponnese. But the Kokytos has been firmly identified with a tributary of the Acheron which rises in the Thesprotian hills between Paramythia and Margarition. Here and there along its short course, which skirts the Acherusian marsh for much of its way, are situations not lacking in charm with fine prospects eastward, across the plain, to the daunting mountains on the other side, flysch rock, sombre and deeply scarred. It is worth tarrying by its confluence with the Acheron in Persephone's grove of poplars and willows.

THE EVENOS

Where Nessos Was Killed

THERE WAS A KING by name Evenos, a son of Ares, whose beautiful daughter Marpessa had many suitors. But her father had a peculiar idiosyncrasy, not uncommon among heroes of those days: that of wanting one's favourite daughter to remain a virgin. So, like another famous hero, Oenomaos, he would organize chariot races in which his daughter's wooers would compete with him personally. Marpessa would be given to the victor. The losers forfeited their lives and were beheaded. As Evenos contrived to be always the winner, the decapitated heads accumulated. Horrified at the sight, Apollo, who had fallen in love with Marpessa, decided to compete. But Idas, son of Poseidon, who was also in love with Marpessa, acted more swiftly. He obtained from his father a winged chariot in which he eloped with the young girl. Evenos followed in desperate pursuit and, being unable to catch up with them, threw himself into the river Lykormas in Aitolia, which henceforth took his name and became identified with him.[1]

Epirus is rich in streams, but further south, in Akarnania, there are practically none apart from the Acheloös which only borders it. Likewise Aitolia is poor in rivers of any note, apart from the Acheloös, with one exception. This is the Evenos, a river of considerable mythological importance. It rises in the slopes of the Mount Korax range of the southern Pindos and flows southward, emptying itself into the Gulf of Corinth.

It is a river of no great length and rather limited volume of water compared with the Acheloös – a mild and in summer rather shallow stream. Nor is it outstanding for natural beauty, but along its course there are several attractive situations which recall its mythological past.

As one goes along the highway from Mesolonghi to Antirhion and crosses the river over a bridge one will notice, especially if one is travelling in the summer, that there is hardly any water in the wide gravelly bed, a scarcity resulting from many little deviations and much pumping for irrigation purposes. A few miles further upstream the river is more plentiful. If one takes a turning to the left and follows the old road, not the newly built stretch of highway that runs further up the hillside, one will come to a grove of great plane trees off the road to the left and close to the river, which at this point is a rushing stream with pools deep enough to swim in on a hot summer day and with oleander in blossom along its banks.

Whereas until a few years ago this grove was frequented only by goatherds and the occasional lorry driver halting for his siesta, nowadays it is invaded during the summer months by tourists and holiday-makers. Nevertheless it still retains something of its numinous character, so that looking out from its leafy shade at the shingly banks of the stream one is led to conjure up the memorable scene in mythology that occurred at a ford of the Evenos somewhere along this stretch of the river (Plate 15).

Herakles, who had won the hand of Deianeira by beating Acheloös in their wrestling contest, was travelling home with her when he came to this ford which was perilous at that time of the year, the river being swollen from the winter rains. The centaur Nessos was the ferryman, or ferry 'monster', who carried travellers across and received payment for his services. Now Herakles felt that he could easily brave the roaring stream and safely carry Deianeira across. Besides, he was well aware of the notoriously lecherous inclinations of centaurs. But Deianeira was a sporting girl[2] and insisted on riding on Nessos's back. She thought it would be much more fun to ride a centaur than to be carried awkwardly across by her husband. So there was an argument between the two. Deianeira had her way and pulled herself up onto the centaur's back without Herakles' help. Nessos, with Deianeira astride, proceeded to cross in a leisurely fashion. Herakles was already on the opposite bank when he noticed that Nessos, still midstream, was making improper advances to his wife. But what was he actually doing?

Apollodoros states that Nessos tried to violate her,[3] and Ovid, in his more embroidered account,[4] seems to imply the same, but I am more inclined to go along with Sophocles whose Deianeira in his *Trachiniae* says that when they were midstream Nessos touched her with wanton hands.[5] Hardly a rape.

What this probably amounted to is very charmingly shown on a sixth-century BC Attic cup – by Ambrosios the vase painter – which is now in the British Museum. We see bearded Nessos turning his head round, kissing and fondling Deianeira. What more could he have done? How can a centaur rape a lady midstream so long as she sits riding on his back? But Herakles was very sensitive and got overexcited, perhaps not entirely without cause, for Deianeira, as depicted by Ambrosios, did not seem to mind being fondled by the centaur. So the incensed hero took his bow and shot Nessos with one of his arrows that had been dipped in the poisonous blood of the Hydra.

11 The Thyamis, rising in the northwestern mountains, is mentioned by Thucidydes, Strabo and other writers. Though no recorded myths about the river have survived, the power of its flow and the sheer beauty of its passage may well have led it to be revered as a river god.

12 The Thyamis, in more tranquil mood after its violent outburst, flows peacefully towards its outlet in the Ionian Sea near Corfu.

13 The Arachthos, the largest river of Epirus, is remarkable for the rounded limestone boulders which abound in its upper reaches. No recorded myths have survived but the river was undoubtedly worshipped as a river god since it was represented as such on local silver coins.

14 The soaring bridge across the Arachthos, built during Ottoman rule in Greece, provides a stark contrast to the Hellenic inspiration of the Epirus landscape of northwestern Greece.

15 The Evenos rises in north-western Greece and flows into the Gulf of Corinth. It takes its name from a jealous king who threw himself into the river after failing to protect the virginity of his daughter, who had eloped with the son of Poseidon.

16 The Peneios, a venerable river god and one of the most prominent of Ancient Greece, was the father of the beautiful but ill-fated nymph Daphne, pursued so tragically by Apollo. The river flows from the Pindos mountains east into the Aegean sea.

Mortally wounded, the centaur managed to cross to the opposite bank where he collapsed. Before dying, with revenge in his heart, he persuaded Deianeira to collect the clotted blood of his poisoned wound and keep it as a charm against any possible infidelity on the part of Herakles. Ovid says that Nessos smeared the blood onto his tunic which he gave to Deianeira for Herakles to put on should the need arise. Sophocles, however, makes no mention of such a tunic and instead tells us that Deianeira stored the collected blood in an urn, using the blood years later to smear on a robe she gave Herakles to wear in order to cure him of his infatuation for another woman; instead, the blood killed him.

Diadorous Siculus adds a lurid touch to the picture of the tragedy by assuming that Nessos was already having intercourse with Deianeira, having presumably reached the other side of the river before Herakles, when he was struck by the arrow. Both he and Apollodoros say that the dying Nessos urged Deianeira to mix the poisoned blood with his sperm which he had dropped on the ground in his sexual excitement – fertile soil for anthropologists to dig in.[6]

Strabo describes the course of river Evenos as follows:

> The Evenus begins in the country of the Ophians, the Ophians being an Aetolian tribe ... and flows at first, not through the Curetan country, which is the same as the Pleuronian, but through the more easterly country, past Calchis and Calydon; and then, bending back towards the plains of old Pleuron and changing its course to the west, it turns towards its outlet and the south. In earlier times it was called the Lycormas. And there Nessus, it is said, who had been appointed ferryman, was killed by Heracles because he tried to violate Deianeira when he was ferrying her across the river.[7]

The valley of the Evenos, which is still fairly green, used to be thickly wooded and in parts well cultivated. Wild boars still roam about, but once upon a time a monstrous and deadly fierce wild boar infested the country. It had been sent by Artemis in her wrath at not having received sacrifices from Oeneos, king of Kalydon, a city in the close neighbourhood of the river. Apollodoros tells us that this boar, of extraordinary strength and size, prevented the land from being sown and destroyed the cattle and the people that fell in with it.[8] Likewise Bakchylides says:

> The Goddess-Maiden's wrath was irresistible, and she sped a wide-mighted boar, shameless in battle, into the lawns of Calydon, where on the flood of his strength he went goring the vine-rows and slaying the sheep together with every man that came athwart his way.[9]

Ovid, in accordance with his style, describes the beast flamboyantly:

> This boar was as big as the bulls found in grassy Epirus, bigger than the Sicilian ones. There was a fiery gleam in its bloodshot eyes, it held its neck high and stiff, its hide bristled with hairs that stuck straight out like spears. It bellowed harshly, the hot foam

23

flecking its broad shoulders, and its teeth were like elephants' tusks; fire issued from its jaws, the leaves were set alight by its breath.[10]

The ruin wrought by this monstrous boar, which ravaged the fertile valley of the Evenos, and the whole neighbourhood of Kalydon, roused to action the king's son, Meleager, who was Deianeira's brother and had taken part in the Golden Fleece expedition. For assistance in his task of killing the boar he appealed to his former Argonaut companions, who answering his call came to him from throughout Greece. So the celebrated Kalydonian boar hunt took place, which Pausanias describes as represented with great artistry by the sculptor Skopas on the pediment of the temple of Tegea.[11] It was also a subject much favoured by Attic vase painters.

Already Homer tells us about the hunt,[12] and after him several poets and mythographers of the ancient world complete the picture. As usual Ovid gives us the most vivid as well as the most florid account.[13] Although the boar was finally slain, after it had wounded and killed several of the hunters, the whole adventure ended in tragedy – a typical ancient Greek tragedy – all because of a woman, Atalanta, who had been the first to wound the boar. With less poetic prolixity than Ovid, Apollodoros goes straight to the heart of the matter, the anti-feminism of those days, which caused the disaster.[14]

Atalanta stands out as one of the most interesting female characters of Greek mythology. She is a perfect specimen of the Artemis type of female which from time to time appears in the ancient world amongst women as well as nymphs. Drawn to adventure and deeds of prowess, or simply in love with horses and hunting, she shuns the company of men or competes with them on equal terms, preferring to remain a virgin, but not necessarily immune to Eros in the end. Foremost among such women were, of course, the Amazons, who mated with men only to acquire daughters, the male offspring being at once suppressed. Probably Deianeira belonged to this category of females before she was softened by marriage to Herakles, if credence is to be given to Apollodoros who states that she drove a chariot and practised the art of war.[15] Atalanta was the embodiment of this type of woman. 'Fair Atalanta,' Hesiod says, 'swift of foot, the daughter of Schonoeneus, who had the beaming eye of the Graces, though she was ripe for wedlock rejected the company of her equals and sought to avoid marriage with men who eat bread.'[16]

This virgin huntress, who competed with men in wrestling matches and was able to beat the famous hero Peleos in one of these contests, had taken part in the Argonaut expedition[17] and so Meleager already knew her when he invited her to join the chase. But whether he had already fallen in love with her on board the *Argo* we are not told. Probably he had. On this occasion, however, his infatuation for her gave rise to a fatal uproar. The award for the hunter who succeeded in killing the boar was to be its hide. Atalanta proved to be the first to wound it, and Meleager, noticing with delight this success, promised her a reward. So when it turned out to be he who finally slew the beast, instead of taking the skin for himself he awarded it to Atalanta. Now Meleager's two uncles on his mother's side, who were taking part in the hunt despite the initial fuss they had made about having to go hunting with a woman, expressed indignation at Meleager's decision. 'Thinking scorn that a woman should get the prize in the face of men, [they] took the skin from her alleging that it belonged to them by right of birth, if Meleager did not choose to take it.' There followed a scuffle, and Meleager 'in a rage slew the sons of Thestios and gave the skin to Atalanta'.[18]

So the Kalydonian hunt ended. A series of further disasters followed culminating in Meleager's own death. But before this happened Atalanta went home to the Peloponnese while Meleager had to face the unforgiving wrath of his mother Althaia, whose brothers he had killed. According to Homer she invoked Persephone and the Erinys to avenge them by bringing death upon her son. Her remaining brothers at the head of their people, the Kuretes, attacked the city of Kalydon and wasted the country. Labouring under his mother's curse Meleager would not defend the city, but finally, persuaded by his wife, he sallied forth and in the battle that ensued killed his two remaining uncles. For Althaia this was the last straw.

On the hearth of the king's palace at Kalydon overlooking the green valley of the Evenos lay once a strange log of wood which, a few days after Meleager's birth, the Fates pointed out to his mother and announced that her son would live only so long as this brand was not consumed by fire. Althaia snatched it up and deposited it in a safe place. But now, incensed by the death of all her brothers at the hand of her son, she took out of the chest the brand 'which the Fates had foretold coeval, in life and death, with her son',[19] and cast it on the fire. Meleager, who was still fighting the Kuretes, felt an inner fire consuming his vitals and died in agony. Thereupon Althaia and Meleager's wife Cleopatra, granddaughter of the river god Evenos, committed suicide.

But what happened to Atalanta? Keen about her virginity though she was, her affair with Meleager had failed to be Platonic. They had indeed made love, probably in the beautiful groves on the Evenos whenever they left off hunting for a rest, and so she bore him a child in accordance with his wishes.[20] On her return to the Peloponnese the child was exposed in the mountains of Arcadia and found there by shepherds who named him Parthenopaios, or 'son of a stricken maidenhead', because Atalanta insisted on being regarded as still a virgin.[21] Of course in those days it was common practice to leave unwanted infants in the mountains for shepherds to find and rear, since there always was a kind-hearted shepherd ready for the task. On the same mountain on which Atalanta abandoned her child in order to go on playing the part of a virgin, she herself had been exposed by her own father Iasos, who wanted to have only male offspring.

Delightful, however, is the story of her life that followed, which is related, with

25

slight variations, by many a poet and mythographer – the story of how her father recognized her as his daughter at last and received her home, insisting, however, on her getting married; how not wanting to marry she disposed of her suitors by competing with them in the foot race and always beating them, whereby they forfeited their lives; how finally Melanion, desperately in love with her and not without some veiled response, was able to win, with the help of Aphrodite, by letting three beautiful apples fall in the course of the race one after the other, which the goddess had given him and which enchanted Atalanta who stooped to pick them up as she ran, and so lost the race by being thus delayed; and how the delights of love softened her, how drawn by the beauty of a shady grove, which as ill luck would have it was sacred to Zeus, she and Melanion made love in it and consequently roused the god's wrath who changed them into lions. But all this takes us away from our river, the Evenos.

From the hills of the city of Kalydon, whose ruins on a prominence off the highway include the foundations of the temple of Artemis, you look down through cornfields into the wide valley of the river. The view is extensive and the landscape cannot fail to arouse visions of a huge, savage boar being hunted down by the heroes of old.

OTHER RIVERS OF NORTHWESTERN GREECE

THERE ARE A NUMBER of rivers in northwestern Greece, mainly in Epirus, which flow with a fairly abundant, as well as constant, volume of water throughout the year, but about which practically no information has come down to us through mythology. Several of them, however, are described – or at least mentioned – by historians and geographers of the ancient world such as Thucydides, Polybius, Strabo and Livy. They deserve some attention not only because they were most probably revered as river gods – the Arachthos without any doubt – but also on account of their natural beauty often in a spectacular setting.

In the far north is the Aoös, which rises in the Pindos mountains northeast of Ioannina and flows westward through virtually uninhabited forests of conifers, between the peaks of Gamela and Smolikas, the highest summits of the Pindos range, out of sight into Albania and eventually into the Adriatic Sea. This is a river of ancient Illyria. It is mentioned by Ovid[1] as one of the river gods that came to console Peneios over the fate of his daughter Daphne, as well as by Polybius in connection with naval and military operations, and by Strabo[2] in connection with the old Corinthian colony of Apollonia situated in its lower reaches not far from the sea. Its course lies well to the north of the ancient world of Greece. Therefore it is not surprising that there are no appertaining myths we know of or are likely to discover. However, it has a tributary, nowadays called the Voidomati, or Ox-eye, which though likewise lacking in recorded myths should be taken into account none the less, because of its great natural beauty.

The Voidomati rises in the dry bottom of the Viko gorge, perhaps the wildest and most magnificent gorge in Europe, a great cleft in the breadlike crust of the Tymphe massif. In this barren scenery, the haunt of former anchorites, the mind boggles at the desolation of nature, at the sight of Titanic shapes, at the immensity of the rock walls that rise sheer above the thirsty roughness of the bottom. Suddenly, out of a mass of dry stones, a fully fledged river wells up, no doubt an underground stream emerging to the surface, fed by the snows of Gamela, Astraka and the other surrounding peaks. Here the Viko gorge ends and at once great trees – oak, kermes, celtis, maple, willow, oriental plane tree and oriental hornbeam – cluster along the Voidomati banks. The blue-green water foaming and sparkling with trout, icy cold, delicious to drink and seductive for a quick dive in the heat of summer, streams along a ravine far lesser than the Viko gorge but impressive nevertheless and much more inviting, though accessible only by wading and scrambling goatlike through brush.

As you proceed down the river in this manner, the symphony of colours and shapes, which the bare red rock surfaces strike up with the varied vegetation of trees, shrubs and herbs, is enhanced by the water rushing between lichen-skinned boulders. The great limestone cliff of Astraka, one of the Tymphe heights, towers sheer in the immediate background, white, pink or russet according to the light, luminous like a marble throne of the gods. Two deserted monasteries and a fine Turkish bridge at the opening of the gorge six or seven miles downstream complete the landscape of this river, which soon joins the Aoös in the plain of Konitsa.

A little more than halfway between the north and the south of Epirus the Thyamis flows, southwestward, emptying itself into the Ionian Sea opposite Corfu. Like the Aoös it is mentioned by Strabo and also by Thucydides and other writers, but lacks any recorded myths. On the drive from Igoumenitsa to Ioannina the traveller cannot fail to take note of it, for the road skirts the left bank from time to time. It is a pleasant river, well shaded by plane trees, which flows through fine though rather sober scenery. Spectacular, however, is the spot where it receives its main supply of water from a spring in a deep glen. The ravine into which it pours, over the edge of a precipice, is extremely steep and about one hundred and twenty feet deep, the sides of it almost sheer but bristling with thick vegetation, kermes shrubs, spina christi, thistles and other thorny growth through which a slippery, prickly, perilous descent can be made to the bottom.[3] The stream, rich in water, roars along this cleft between great boulders and gnarled plane trees. The boulders are of flysch rock, therefore essentially dark grey or brown, but mostly covered with different kinds of moss that vary in their shades of green (Plate 11). The boulders surge out of the roaring white foam, spotted and mottled beasts about to move, like leopards emerging from prehistory. A great arch of stone, almost a dome, rises high above you, spanning the ravine. You find yourself in a natural cathedral, with water thundering and spouting down the nave which is festooned with creepers, their leaves catching the sunbeams that break in, and glittering like tinsel against the deep shadows of overhanging rock. The architectural character of the site, the rich vegetation and rushing water create an ensemble of beauty unique in the whole of Greece, awe-inspiring, numinous. Indeed it compares favourably with a very few similar situations such as the Lousios, the Neda and the Lymax provide in the Peloponnese. After its turbulent outburst the Thyamis winds its way gently down to the sea under the rustling leaves of plane trees (Plate 12).

South of the Thyamis is another river worth noting which is totally ignored, however, by ancient writers including Strabo. This is the Louros, which from a deep blue pool on the lower slopes of Mount Tomaros flows southward through a narrow gorge into the Ambrakian Gulf. Like the Thyamis it is flanked by a highroad for much of its course and so, on the way from Ioannina to Arta, one cannot help being aware of its shady banks. It is in no way outstanding as a stream but it is noteworthy for two reasons: because of its delightful source, a small lake off the main road to the west, a couple of miles before the defile starts, and because of the magnificent remains of the Roman aquaduct further down the gorge, which supplied with water Nikopolis, the city built by the emperor Augustus near the site of his naval victory over Antony. Piranesi-like the pillars and arches bedecked with creepers leap up from the river among splendid plane trees and glistening pools. A spring of gorgeously abundant water gushes out of the bare rock on the left bank and comes pouring into the stream.

Of all the rivers of Epirus the Arachthos, or Aratthus, as it is sometimes trans-literated, is the largest and from the point of view of natural beauty the most striking, the Acheron being a much more modest stream and the Acheloös scarcely an Epirotan river since it only skirts the border of the region for a brief tract.

The Arachthos is not lacking in references to it by ancient writers, in particular Polybius, Strabo and Livy, on account of its strategic importance, inasmuch as it flows past the walls of the ancient capital of Epirus, Ambrakia now Arta, for a few miles before emptying itself into the Ambrakian gulf. Though no recorded myths relating to it have come down to us, it was undoubtedly worshipped as a river god, for as such it is represented, in various forms, on ancient Ambrakian silver coins. There must, therefore, have been relevant myths in the locality, and indeed parts of the river course are still intensely evocative of their mythological past.

According to Strabo, the Arachthos rises on Mount Tymphe. Its source is in actual fact situated in a glen of the Mount Tymphe region, not so very far from where the Aoös rises. It flows southward, east of the Ioannina lake, through a deep gorge in magnificent limestone country. The remarkable character of the scenery is enhanced by the Zoumerka peaks of the Pindos, which soar above the Arachthos in dramatic shapes to heights of about eight thousand feet. This great jagged crest of limestone runs longitudinally, with the Acheloös flowing along the base of its east side and the Arachthos along that of its west side, twin rivers as it were, though one is much shorter than the other, rushing and roaring through clefts and chasms.

The Arachthos is particularly remarkable for the nature of the boulders in certain

29

stretches of its course (Plate 13). Having detached themselves from the overhanging cliffs and dropped or rolled into the river, they have been subjected to the action of the rushing water for millennia, which of course is the history of boulders in every mountain stream that flows through rocky ravines. But in the Arachthos gorge, on account of the geological nature of the rock, the boulders, abraded into pieces of sculpture, smoothed and polished by the current, show up their quality of stone which is almost crystallized and thus very close to marble. They shine dazzling white in the sun in contrast to the deep blue-green of the water and the velvety indented green of the overhanging plane leaves, the predominant vegetation. With these and other elements they engage in a play of colours and light effects, the resulting atmosphere, the *religio loci*, almost totally sequestered, being intensely numinous. Each boulder retains its individual shape and place, as each tree its personality with its roots pushing right into the stone and often entwining whole rocks, and yet every part of the close-up landscape is interdependent and in harmony with the whole. Like the Acheron this is a scenery in which every detail of the foreground and immediate background draws your attention without your ceasing to be aware that they all belong to a whole on a magnificent scale – a great gorge with a monastery clinging perilously, like a medieval castle, to the edge of a precipitous cliff. The lack, otherwise, of architecture or houses of any sort in what is a virtually uninhabited region is here no deficiency or im-perfection, for in the waters of the Arachthos, as on the banks of the Acheron, the rock has been given by nature the role that architecture plays where the presence of fine buildings is appreciated as part of the landscape. In the setting of both these rivers the rock has been shaped not only into sculptural but also into architectural forms. On the Acheron the banks have been given sharp, angular and perpendicular interrelated shapes; in the waters of the Arachthos the boulders of practically the same limestone have been rounded into female limbs, caressed and licked by a river god.

II

EASTERN
GREECE

EAST OF THE Pindos range, from the Thracian mountains of Haimos and Rhodope southward to Boeotia and Attica, lie many more regions of Greece than west of the Pindos. Their ancient culture was virtually autochthonous, especially south of Makedonia, where the area was an integral part of Greece. Their rivers are rich in myths, many records of which have survived, though not all. Most of these rivers rise either in the Pindos range and its southern offshoots, flowing eastward and southeastward, or in the Thracian mountains of the north and beyond, in non-Grecian territories, flowing southward into the Aegean Sea. Of course, they were all river gods, the most important being Peneios, Axios, Strymon, Spercheios, Kephisos, Asopos and, right down south, Ilissos and Attic Kephisos.

6

THE PENEIOS AND ITS TRIBUTARIES

Daphne's Father

Phoebus, of you even the swan sings with clear voice to the beating of his wings, as he alights upon the bank by the eddying river Peneius.[1]

BEFORE COMING TO Apollo and his close association with the Peneios, one of the most prominent river gods of ancient Greece, mentioned by Hesiod in his list of great rivers, the son of Okeanus and Tethys,[2] let us seek out the river's source high up in the Pindos mountains where it is to be found not far from Aspripigi, the spring of the Acheloös, likewise on the eastern declivities of Mount Lakmon.

There may still be swans singing and beating their wings on the banks of these rivers, but are there lions, bears and wolves? The traveller may well ask as he looks down from the Pindos heights into Makedonia and Thessaly, recalling what the ancient writers wrote. According to Aristotle,[3] lions still roamed these regions. As he was born at Stageira in northern Greece and was closely associated with the royal house of Makedon, it is unlikely that he was blindly repeating what Herodotus had said. The historian tells us that lions were to be found in the stretch of country between the river Nestos in Thrace and the Acheloös, but nowhere else in Europe, and that they attacked the camels of Xerxes' invading army.[4]

The lions have departed long ago, but there are still bears in the Pindos, so the Vlach shepherds say, but more numerous and troublesome than the bears are the wolves which account for the savage dogs that attack the traveller in quest of river

33

springs. The shepherds will tell the traveller that they have to keep these dogs to protect their sheep from the wolves. And there, in a forest of conifers, where there are bears and wolves, is the source of the Peneios, a sparkling spring pouring out of the rock, embedded in moss and foliage, from which the river flows down the valley into the plain of Thessaly past the Meteora pinnacles.

Surrounded on all sides by hills and mountains, the plain of Thessaly is a flat basin which must have been a lake once upon a time, for the eminences within and around it rise abruptly from total flatness, thereby giving the scenery its characteristic feature. The brilliant geographical account of Thessaly given to us by Herodotus, whose capacity for accurate observation and rational deduction seldom fail, is well worth quoting here in full because of the relevant fluvial context:

> There is a tradition that Thessaly was in ancient times a lake, shut in on every side by huge hills. Ossa and Pelion – ranges which join at the foot – do in fact enclose it upon the east, while Olympus forms a barrier upon the north, Pindus upon the west, and Othrys towards the south. The tract contained within these mountains, which is a deep basin, is called Thessaly. Many rivers pour their waters into it; but five of them are of more note than the rest, namely the Peneius, the Apidanus, the Onochonos, the Enipius and the Pamisus. These streams flow down from the mountains which surround Thessaly, and meeting in the plain, mingle their waters together, and discharge themselves into the sea by a single outlet, which is a gorge of extreme narrowness. After the junction all the other names disappear, and the river is known as the Peneius. It is said that of old the gorge which allows the waters an outlet did not exist; accordingly the rivers, which were then, as well as the Lake Boebeis, without name, but flowed with as much waters as at present, made Thessaly a sea. The Thessalians tell us that the gorge through which the water escapes was caused by Poseidon; and this is likely enough; at least any man who believes that Poseidon causes earthquakes, and that chasms so produced are his handiwork, would say, upon seeing this rent, that Poseidon did it. For it plainly appeared to me that the mountains had been torn asunder by an earthquake.[5]

Strabo says more or less the same thing, but his geographical description is not nearly so graphic.

The Peneios winds its way through the Thessalian plain bordered by willows, poplars, and plane trees (Plate 16), but its waters are far from clear, for they take some of the substance of the loamy soil of the plain through which they flow and hence much of its colour. However, on entering the cleft in the mountains described by Herodotus, the famous Vale of Tempe, which is about seven kilometres in length and through the ages has fascinated poets and travellers, the river becomes much greener as it flows under the foliage of great plane trees (Plate 16). Tempe, 'the trees' or 'the woods' as the term originally meant, is indeed an appropriate name for this shady defile. But at present the paths down to the river from the motorway, which runs through the gorge, are deprived, by the uncontrolled requirements of tourism, of that

34

poetry which had happily endured for so many centuries. Until about the beginning of the twentieth century there was no more than a rough track for the traveller on his way through the gorge.

The Vale of Tempe has been described by many. Pliny gives us a glorified picture of it, wallowing in it, a picture that shows how far the fantasy of a writer could be stirred by the sheer image that myths and poets create beyond the facts and features of the real scenery. He says that there are gently sloping hills rising beyond human sight on either side

> ... while the valley between is verdant with a grove of trees. Along it glides the Peneius, glittering with pebbles and adorned with grassy banks, melodious with the choral song of birds. Into it flows the river Orcus, which it hardly receives but merely carries it for a brief space floating on its surface like a skin of oil, in Homer's phrase, and then rejects it refusing to allow the punitive waters engendered for the service of the Furies to mingle with its silvery flood.[6]

There are not and never were any gentle hills in the Tempe gorge where only awesome red, yellow and ochre cliffs rise sheer to impressive heights. The Peneios glides along not silvery but muddy green, without pebbles and with hardly any grass on its banks, but shaded, however, by fine plane trees. As for melodious birds, there are only magpies cawing in summer, though nightingales can be heard in the spring. The river Pliny calls Orkos is the Titaressos of Homer which nowadays has practically no water in the summer, probably because of irrigation. In Homer's day it may have been more plentiful. In listing the ships and people that gathered in support of Agamemnon's expedition, Homer says:

> And Gouneus led from Cyphus two and twenty ships, and with him followed Enienes and the Peraebi, staunch in fight, that had set their dwellings about wintry Dodona, and dwelt in the ploughland about lovely Titaressus, that poureth his fair-flowing streams into Peneius; yet doth he not mingle with the silvery eddies of Peneius, but floweth on over his waters like unto olive oil; for that he is a branch of the water of Styx, the dreaded river of oath.[7]

Homer may have meant the opposite of Pliny's assumption in this strange account of the confluence of the two rivers, for the water of the Styx is indeed pure and transparent, and so would reject for a while the murkier water of the Peneios. I have seen something of the kind in the Peloponnese, where the extremely clear stream of the rushing Lousios succeeds in thrusting aside the muddy waters of the Alpheios for some length of its course as the two rivers come together and merge. Eventually, however, the Lousios is submerged by the darker waters of the Alpheios, whose cloudy whirls advance expanding from bank to bank.

Livy has left us a better and in a way more vivid picture of the Vale of Tempe than

35

either Pliny or Aelian whose description is likewise mellow and florid. Aelian's description runs as follows:

> In a region between Olympus and Ossa the mountains are of extraordinary height and disjoined by divine action, as it would seem, a gap having been made which extends in length for forty stadia, broad about one plethrum [100 yards] in some places and somewhat more in others. Along the middle runs the river Peneios into which other rivers flow thus making it great. It affords various places of all kinds not wrought by the hand of man, but spontaneously by nature which from the very first delighted in embellishing the place and contributing to its splendour and fame. Ivy full of down abounds here which, like the generous vine, entwines the high trees and grows with them. There is also plenty of smallage [smylax] on the banks of the river. Climbing up the hillside it covers the rocks which lie thus hidden, nothing being seen but the green carpet of the herb, a real pleasure to the eye. The vale is full of delightful groves and caves which in the summer provide the traveller with shelter and refreshing rest. It abounds in little brooks and springs of water cool and pleasant to the taste. These waters, it is said, are beneficial to whoever bathes in them, being extremely invigorating. The most melodious birds keep singing everywhere and delight the traveller as he goes by. The pleasant places of rest I have mentioned lie on either side of the river Peneios, which flows through the vale of Tempe smoothly and gently like oil. The trees that border the banks provide much shade with their thick foliage which, for the greater part of the day, keeps off the sunbeams, thus affording a cool passage for those that sail. From the entire neighbourhood people gather here to offer sacrifices, converse and hold festivities. As offerings are being made and perfumes burnt the whole time the traveller on foot or by water cannot help breathing the most delicious smells. The constant worship of the gods that goes on makes the place sacred.[8]

Livy's account is not only shorter but also more matter-of-fact and succinct. The picture he gives us stands out in sharp contrast to Aelian's.

> Even without opposition of an enemy Tempe is a defile difficult of passage; for besides five miles of narrows through which the road is cramped for a loaded animal, the cliffs on either side are so sheer that one can hardly look down without some dizziness of eye and brain. An additional source of fear is the roar and the depth of the Peneius river flowing through the midst of the canyon. This place, so unfriendly by its nature, was blocked at four separate points by the king's garrisons.

But even Livy falls short of complete accuracy since the Peneios never roared but has always flowed peacefully and silently.

When, from the end of the eighteenth century, travellers started visiting the Vale of Tempe on account of its fame in antiquity, the first such visitor being the Swede Björstähls, they were shocked to find that the vale was not a vale, but a forbidding gorge. Björstähls was followed a few years later by Hawkins who in 1797 explored the area thoroughly and then concluded the description he made with the following comment:

36

It is scarcely necessary for me to add, that the scenery itself by no means corresponds with the idea that has been generally conceived of it; and that the eloquence of Aelian has given rise to expectations which the traveller will not find realized. In the fine description which the writer has given of Tempe, he seems to have misconceived the general character of the scenery, which is distinguished by an air of savage grandeur, rather than by its beauty and amenity, the aspect of the whole defile impressing the spectator with a sense of danger and difficulty, not of security and indulgence. In short it is mortifying to be obliged to confess that the highly finished picture which Aelian has left us of Tempe is almost wholly an imaginary one: and that even those that are sketched with so much force by Livy and Pliny bear no very marked resemblence.[9]

In spite of this shock Hawkins does concede much beauty to the river Peneios as it flows through its gorge, for elsewhere in his account he says this:

The full but silent stream of that river is bordered nearly in all its course through the dell by the oriental plane tree, which support the wild vine thickly interlaced among its branches and dropping in festoons to the surface of the water. This beautiful parasite was at the season when I visited Tempe in full bloom, and scented the air with a delightful odour. About midway a fountain of the coldest water gushes out at the foot of a rock, which forms the base of the causeway. Here travellers usually halt to refresh themselves and their cavalry; while many repose here, or devour, as we did, the contents of their wallets, cooling their wine in the crystal fountain.

If Hawkins was shocked to find that the Tempe he saw was so different from the picture left to us by the ancient Greek and Latin writers, what would he say if he could see the touristified 'vale' of today, two hundred years after his visit? And what would be said by Dodwell, who visited Tempe early in the nineteenth century and wrote:

The wild olive, the laurel, the oleander, the agnos, various kinds of arbuti, the yellow jasmine, terebinth, lentiscus and rosemary, with myrtle and laburnum, richly decorate the margin of the river, while masses of aromatic plants and flowers exhale their varied perfume and breathe their luscious odours through the scented air.[10]

Cooped between the railway on its left bank and the motorway on its right, the Peneios flows on, still shaded by plane trees (Plate 20). But the deafening noise of traffic on the tarmac road, where huge lorries and an unbroken stream of cars tear along at high speed, the crowded car-parks provided for the visitors who halt to step down to the river, the numerous gift shops and restaurants catering for package-tour groups as well as for local holiday-makers, the muddy banks strewn with plastic bags and other human refuse through which the traveller wades in a hopeless search for some bay foliage sacred to Apollo, have created a situation in which it is hard to find, or even feel, any trace of those elements that in the past kept the traveller spellbound.

Apollo's connection with the Peneios is undoubtedly very ancient. From Homer through the ages, references to the river in relation to the god by poets and mythographers are not lacking. Two were the nymphs very close to the river god, being related to him. One was Kyrene, the river god's granddaughter with whom Apollo eloped to North Africa. The other, according to a much later tradition, was Daphne, daughter of Peneios, with whom Apollo was less successful.

There is a beautiful Pythian Ode of Pindar[11] in which he tells us how Apollo carried off the maiden huntress Kyrene from the windswept glens of Mount Pelion where lived her father Hypseos, whose mother was the naiad Kreusa, 'the happy bride of the river god Peneios'. Virgil, in relating the life of Kyrene's son by Apollo, Aristaios, creates an idyllic picture of her dwelling at the very source of the Peneios, surrounded and attended by nymphs.[12] The river god's own dwelling, on the other hand, is described by Ovid in no less fanciful terms:

> There is a vale in Thessaly which steep-wooded slopes surround on every side. Men call it Tempe. Through this the Peneius flows from the foot of Pindos with foam-like waters, and by its heavy fall forms clouds which drive along fine, smoke-like mist, sprinkles the tops of trees with spray, and deafens even remoter regions by its roar. Here is the home, the seat, the inmost haunt of the mighty stream. Here, seated in a cave of overhanging rock, he was giving laws to his waters and to his nymphs.[13]

The myth of Daphne, the nymph pursued by Apollo and changed into a laurel tree on the banks of the Peneios, has become well known in the Western world through Ovid. His account inspired many a Renaissance and Baroque artist, some very prominent, such as Pollaiuolo (Plate 17) and Bernini (Plate 18). Indeed one of the most vivid passages of the *Metamorphoses*[14] deals with this story at length, the story of Peneios' daughter obdurately dedicated to virginity despite her father's objections, who flees Apollo though he is passionately in love with her. She is depicted as borne by the winds in her flight, her garments set in a flutter by opposing currents of air, her hair flung and flowing behind her in a light breeze. Apollo keeps on pursuing her as she runs desperately along the banks of the Peneios. Finally she cries out to her father for help, which does not fail to come, but arrives in the form of her gradual transformation into a laurel tree. As he catches up with her, Apollo can still feel her heart flutter beneath the bark. There follows, in Ovid's account, Apollo's declaration of the glorious part that laurel wood and laurel leaves would always play in times to come.

This myth, however, is of relatively late vintage – Hellenistic probably. None of the early, or even classical Greek poets and mythographers mention it, nor do we find it depicted on sixth- and fifth-century BC Attic vases where so many other myths are represented. Not even in Apollodoros and in Diadorous Siculus do we find any reference to Daphne. Where did Ovid get his story from? Not only does the myth emerge late, but it manifests itself also as a typical case in which regional rivalries play their part, somewhat confusing the picture. We have Daphne as daughter of the river god Ladon

17 Daphne, pursued and caught by the love-struck Apollo, was turned into a laurel tree after she appealed to her father, the river god Peneios, for help. The myth inspired many a Renaissance artist including Pollaiuolo, whose painting is shown here. (© National Gallery, London)

18 The myth of Daphne and Apollo, captured here in the Baroque sculpture of Bernini, has had an enduring impact on Western art and mythography.

19 Peneios, the river god, depicted here in a print based on Giulio Romano's painting, is consoled about the fate of his daughter by other river gods.

20 The Peneios, flowing through the Vale of Tempe, is bordered by lush aromatic foliage which has helped to secure through the ages its fame for beauty. It was the laurel trees on the banks on the Peneios which fed the myth of Daphne's fate.

according to Pausanias,[15] Daphne as daughter of Amyklas, king of Sparta, according to Parthenios,[16] and Daphne as daughter of Peneios according to Ovid.

No doubt the custom of crowning the Pythian victors with laurel leaves antedated the appearance of the Daphne myth. The sweet bay tree, or laurel, grew on the banks of the Peneios and was sacred to Apollo before he fell in love with the nymph, before her metamorphosis, or in other words before all this took shape in mythology. Apollo cut a branch from the sacred laurel in the Vale of Tempe and planted it at the side of the Kastalian spring of Delphi. Likewise before the emergence of the Daphne myth the custom at Delphi had most likely already established itself for a mission of well-born youths to be sent to Tempe every nine years, accompanied by flute players, in order to cut a laurel branch and bring it back with them.

The part that the laurel from Tempe played at Delphi is reflected in a charming poem by Kallimachos which consists of an animated dialogue between the bay tree and the olive tree, each upholding its qualities and virtues against the other. Kallimachos was writing at the beginning of the third century BC and makes no mention of Daphne, but his bay tree boastfully says:

> What house is there where I am not beside the doorpost? What seer or sacrificer carries me not with him? Yea, the Pythian priestess has her seat on laurel, laurel she sings and laurel has she for her bed. … And I go to feasts and Pythian dances, and am made a prize of victory. The Dorians cut me on the hill-tops of Tempe and carry me to Delphi, whenever the holy rites of Apollo are celebrated.[17]

Of the four tributaries of the Peneios that Herodotus mentions,[18] only the Enipeus and the Apidamos are worth taking into account, the other two having become insignificant streams, dry in the summer, no doubt largely because of irrigation. Perhaps also the climate has changed. Even in the days of Herodotus, the Onochonos must have been a very modest river since it was one of those that were drunk dry by the army of Xerxes. The Apidamos, which still flows with some water throughout the year, scarcely sufficed their needs.

The Enipeus, which rises in the foothills of Mount Othrys and joins the Peneios a few miles west of Larissa, bears the same name as that of a tributary of the Alpheios in Elis, probably the Lestenitsa of today, west of Olympia. It remains uncertain which of these two rivers was the river god who became deeply involved with Tyro, daughter of Salmoneos, who fell in love with him. As it seems more likely that it was the Elis river, which at any rate is Strabo's view,[19] I shall leave this myth to be dealt with when we come to that region of the Peloponnese.

39

7

THE HALIAKMON, THE AXIOS, THE STRYMON AND THE NESTOS

MOUNT OLYMPUS, the abode of the gods, towers majestically to the northeast of Thessaly. It is strange that this lofty massif should not have provided for a number of rivers with plentiful water to flow from its snows and springs into the Thessalian plain. But if from the Peneios we turn to the north, apart from the insignificant Titaressos there is nothing for us to do but to move on, into the plains and open valleys of Makedonia where some large rivers flow, mythologically noteworthy. Except the Haliakmon, however, they flow for much of their course in Yugoslavia or Bulgaria, so we cannot regard them as exclusively Greek in a geographical sense. But from a mythological point of view they come within the Greek context, as for instance the Skamander in Mysia does.

The Haliakmon flows entirely within Greek geographical territory and is listed by Hesiod in his *Theogony* as one of the divine rivers, the offspring of Okeanos and Tethys.[1] But, as far as I know, no myths connected with it have survived. Strabo mentions it several times, but only from a geographical point of view.[2]

The Haliakmon is a large river without any distinctive features. It could be anywhere in Europe. The same applies to the other Makedonian rivers, as well as the Thracian, but the Axios and the Strymon were river gods of importance in mythology and history.

The Axios, which flows southward from Yugoslavia and empties itself into the Thermaic gulf, is indeed a large river of turbid water. But looking back some millenia into the world of mythology we find it beautifully clear, playing its part as a river god in the *Iliad*. 'The fairest of rivers over the face of the earth',[3] Homer calls it. As a river god Axios did not refrain, of course, from intimate intercourse with women and nymphs, which was followed by consequent offspring. Indeed the hero Pelagon 'was begotten by wide-flowing Axius and Periboea, eldest of the daughters of Acanameus, for with her lay the deep-eddying river'.[4]

Strabo objects to Homer calling it 'most fair', for he found it muddy, and goes out of his way to explain what he thought the Poet really meant.[5] To me its water seemed very much like that of any large Central European river, no bluer than the Danube but no muddier.

A few miles east of the Axios there flows, more or less parallel, the Echeidoros, the present-day Gallikos, which according to Herodotus was one of the rivers drunk dry by the invading army of Xerxes. It cannot have been very plentiful then, but it is certainly a wretched stream now, in the summer consisting only of muddy puddles of water here and there. It has presumably suffered from the irrigation and development schemes of Thessalonika's neighbourhood. No doubt in the days of Xerxes there was more water in it, and more pleasant water to be drunk dry.

Away to the east of Thessalonika and Chalkidike is another great river, which formed the original eastern border of Makedonia. This is the Strymon, broad and deep. Like the Axios its entire upper course lies in a region north of the present-day frontier of Greece, namely in Bulgaria where it is called the Struma; it rises on what was known in the ancient world as Mount Haimos. Thrace was then without definite boundaries, and as time went by came more and more within the orbit of Greece. For the poets and mythographers the Strymon was a prominent river god, and the ancient historians and geographers keep mentioning it in their writings for other reasons as well. First we find Hesiod including it in his list of rivers.[6] Then we have Euripides. Referring to the hero Rhesos, in his drama of that name, he says: 'He comes from Thrace, the river Strymon's son.'[7] Rhesos's mother was the muse Enterpe. Diomedes slew Rhesos at Troy.[8]

Apollodoros tells us that 'Argos received the kingdom and called it the Peloponnese Argos after himself; and having married Evadne, daughter of Strymon and Neaera, he begat Ebasos, Piras, Epidauros and Kriasos who also succeeded to the kingdom.'[9] Strymon's offspring were evidently plentiful.

Further on, Apollodoros informs us thus:

Heracles in his tenth labour entrusted the kine[10] to Hephaestus and hurried away in search of the bull.[11] He found it in the herd of Eryx, and when the king refused to surrender it unless Heracles should beat him in a wrestling bout, Heracles beat him thrice and killed him in the wrestling, and taking the bull drove it with the rest of the

41

herd to the Ionian sea. But when he came to the creeks of the sea, Hera afflicted the cows with a gadfly and dispersed them amongst the skirts of the mountains of Thrace. Heracles went in pursuit and having caught some, drove them to the Hellespont, but the remainder were henceforth wild. Having with difficulty collected the cows, Heracles blamed the river Strymon, and whereas it had been navigable before, he made it unnavigable by filling it with rocks; and he conveyed the kine and gave them to Eurystheus, who sacrificed them to Hera.[12]

The north wind, icy Boreas, was felt to blow down the valley of the Strymon from the snowcapped peaks of northern Thrace. In his Hymn to Apollo, Kallimachos praises the defence of Delos, strong against the blast of winds because of protecting Apollo: 'What defence is there more steadfast? Walls of stone may fall before the blast of Strymonian Boreas, but a god is unshaken forever.'[13] Evidently the Strymon valley formed a sort of funnel through which the north wind blew down into Greece, and in winter the river often froze over. A dramatic picture of how this could affect a rash and unprepared crossing by an army is given to us by Aeschylus in *The Persians*. The messenger, who brings back to the queen mother of Persia news of the disastrous defeat of Xerxes' forces and describes the painful retreat of the army's remnants, in which he himself took part, says this in the course of his account:

> And we came to the Magnesian land and the country of the Macedonians, to the ford of the Axius and Bolbe's ready fens, and to Mount Pangaion, in the Edonian land. But on that night the god roused winter before its time and froze the stream of Sacred Strymon from shore to shore; and many a man who ere that had held the gods in no esteem, implored them then in supplication as he worshipped earth and heaven. But when our host had made an end of its fervent invocation of the gods, it ventured to pass across the ice-bound stream. And whosoever of us started on his way before the beams of the sun-god were dispersed abroad, found himself in safety; for the bright orb of the sun with its burning rays heated the mid-passage and pierced it with flames. One upon another our men sank in, and fortunate indeed was he whose breath of life was sundered soonest.[14]

The waters of the Strymon may indeed be cold, though I didn't test their temperature with a plunge, even though it was June when I tarried on its banks. It is one of the few rivers of Greece in which I haven't swum. The look of it from its famous crossing at the Nine Ways, though impressive, didn't appear to me particularly inviting. Nor have I ever tasted any of its eels, for which it was famous in ancient times. 'And a certain river, famed in the reports of men, that waters the Thracians, shall give its name to thee – the Strymon rich in eels of the largest size,' declared Antiphanes quoted by Athenaios.[15]

A few miles before the Strymon empties itself into the Aegean Sea it almost encircles a hill on which Amphipolis stood, an Athenian colony which held an important strategic position where roads met and crossed – the Ἐννέα ὁδοί, or Nine Ways.[16] It surrendered to the Spartans in the Peloponnesian War in spite of Athenian assistance headed by the historian Thucydides, at that time a general.[17] Little remains of the ancient city, but from the site on the hilltop there is a magnificent view over the surrounding country, with the Strymon winding its way to the sea whose wide horizon stretches out to the south. The buttresses of Mount Pangaion, famous for its gold mines which were a source of wealth to the Makedonian kings, rear themselves over to the east.

The Nine Ways had always been an important strategic point on the banks of the Strymon. Long before Amphipolis was founded, Xerxes and his invading army were brought to a temporary halt here. Strange sacrifices had to be offered to the river god to propitiate him before they could cross the stream. In the seventh book of his history Herodotus tells us:

> The country in the neighbourhood of Mount Pangaeon is known as Phyllis; it extends westward to the Angites, a stream which flows into the Strymon, and southward as far as the Strymon itself. The latter river the Magi tried to propitiate by a sacrifice of white horses, and after performing many other magical tricks in the hope of winning the river's favour, they crossed it at the bridges they found at the Nine Ways, a place in the territory of the Edoni; and when they learnt that Nine Ways was the name of the place, they took nine native boys and nine girls and buried them alive there. Burying people alive is a Persian custom.[18]

About seventy miles to the east, beyond the Pangaion massif, flows the Nestos, which Hesiod calls 'Nessus' in his catalogue of rivers. Like the Strymon it rises in the mountains of northern Thrace and flows for part of its course in Bulgaria. No myths connected with it have come down to us. It is mentioned, however, by Herodotus,[19] Aristotle,[20] Pliny[21] and Pausanias[22] as forming the eastern limit of the region where lions were to be found. Pausanias says: 'The Thracian mountains up country from the river Nestus, which runs through the territory of Abdera, are stocked with beasts including lions.'

Until the fourth century BC the Strymon had formed the eastern boundary of Makedonia, but Philip II and Alexander the Great extended Makedonian territory as far as the Nestos which, as Strabo tells us, became the new boundary with Thrace.[23]

The Nestos was well known for frequently flooding its neighbourhood. Theophrastos says that it often altered its course and 'in so doing caused a growth of forest in that region that by the third year it cast a thick shade'.[24]

8

THE SPERCHEIOS LOVED BY ACHILLES AND ITS TRIBUTARIES

Fifty were the swift ships which Achilles, dear to Zeus, led to Troy, and on each ship at the thole-pins were fifty men, his comrades; and five leaders had he appointed in whom he trusted to give command, and himself in his great might was king over all. One rank was led by Menesthius of the flashing corslet, son of Spercheius, the heaven-fed river. Him did Polydora, daughter of Peleus, bear to tireless Spercheius, a woman couched with a god.[1]

To THE SOUTH of Thessaly, over the hills and mountains of Phtiotis which formed part of the kingdom of Peleos and were later known as Achaia of Phtiotis, the country of Malis opens out in a broad valley in which the river Spercheios flows eastward to the Euboean gulf. The whole region, including the rocky buttresses and footskirts of Mount Oeta, known as the Trachian cliffs, is full of historical and mythological content. The physical outlines of the Achilles and Herakles sagas loom magnificently in this ancient landscape.

The heaven-fed river rises away to the west in the slopes of Mount Tymphrestos, a limestone peak which surges to a height of over seven thousand feet above wooded hills of schist and flysch rock country. The green valley in which it flows is pleasant

and not without grandeur, for Mount Oeta to the south is a feature that gives vigour
to the otherwise sober, if not languid, scenery. The river, however, is not impressive.
'Heaven-fed' no doubt it is, but one might wish it to be more plentifully fed. Except
in its uppermost reaches where there are some charming spots, it has no boulders, its
incline being gentle, and in summer there is not much water throughout its course of
about fifty miles. Of course one should bear in mind that irrigation tends to deplete
it nowadays. Only as it approaches the sea to within a few miles of its outlet in the
Malian gulf, does it deepen thanks to the water of several tributaries. The river is
bordered, however, with poplars, willows and plane trees along most of its banks[1]
(Plate 21). In fact one is inclined here to conjure up both the part it played in the
kingdom of Peleos and the love scenes in which the river god's charm overcame
princesses and nymphs. Indeed he fathered considerable offspring including Phtios
who ruled over Phtiotis, the country to which he gave his name before the days of
Peleos.[2]

The most vivid picture we have of the Spercheios's place and role in the mythical
world is given to us by Homer in the *Iliad*, where Achilles, mourning over Patroklos'
death, expresses not only his grief but his veneration for the river:

> He took his stand apart from the pyre and shore off a golden lock, the rich growth
> whereof he had nursed for the river Spercheius, and, his heart mightily moved, he
> spake: 'Spercheius, to no purpose did my father Peleus vow to thee that when I had
> come home thither to my dear native land, I would shear my hair to thee and offer a
> holy hecatomb, and on the selfsame spot would sacrifice fifty rams, males without
> blemish, into thy waters, where is the demesne of thy fragrant altar. So vowed that old
> man, but thou did not fulfil for him his desire. Now, therefore, seeing I go not home to
> my dear native land, I would fain give to the warrior Patroclus this lock to fare with
> him.'[3]

The above passage is particularly interesting, for it shows that the custom of men,
particularly young men, cutting off locks of their hair and offering them to river gods
was very ancient. Other references to this practice are to be found in Greek literature
and mythology.[4]

'Where the Spercheius waters the plain with kindly stream',[5] as it approaches the
Malian gulf, to the south the cliffs of Trachis rear themselves, on which the acropolis
of Herakleia of Trachis once stood, a city colonized by the Spartans in the fifth century.
Herodotus describes the region, as you approach it from the north, in the following
terms:

> The country round this is flat – broad in one part, very narrow in another; all around
> is a chain of lofty and trackless mountains, called the cliffs of Trachis, which enclose the
> whole territory of Malis. As one comes from Achea, the first town on the bay is Anticyra,
> near which is the mouth of the Spercheius, a river which comes down from the country
> of the Enianes. Some three and a half miles further on there is another river, the Dyras,

45

which according to the legend, burst from the ground to help Heracles when he was burning (Plate 22); then at about the same distance, is another stream, the Melas, and rather more than half a mile beyond that is the town of Trachis. At Trachis the flat ground between the hills and the sea is more extensive than anywhere else, being some half dozen miles across. South of Trachis is a cleft in the mountain range; through it the river Asopus issues and follows a course along the base of the rising ground.[6]

Herodotus' description of the area is fairly accurate, but since his days the plain has been extended for some miles by the silt which the Spercheios and other streams have brought down little by little. The sea of the gulf is now further away and the strategic position of the Thermopylai, a few miles east of Herakleia, has radically changed. Evidently the Asopos and the Dyras were not tributaries of the Spercheios in those days, but flowed straight into the sea. The cleft in the mountains referred to by Herodotus, through which the Asopos comes down into the plain, is a magnificent limestone gorge, desolate and awesome, but the river itself is in the summer a very insignificant stream a few inches deep, hardly worthy of the grandeur in which its course is set.

Noteworthy is Herodotus' reference to Herakles in connection with the river Dyras, for the whole region is saturated with the world of Herakles' last stage of life. Much of this was used by Sophocles as subject matter for his drama *Trachiniae*; the scene is Herakles' home at Trachis where he lived with his family, but from which he had absented himself to fight King Eurytos.[7]

The death of Herakles resulted from the disastrous mistake his wife, Deianeira, made by sending him a robe besmeared with Nessos' blood in the belief that, if he wore it, it would cure him of his infatuation (see page 23). Having heard that he had now fallen in love with Iole, daughter of Eurytos whom he had vanquished and slain in Euboea, and that he intended to marry her, she had recourse to the centaur's recommended remedy, being ignorant of the deceit, for the blood contained the hydra's deadly poison. So Herakles, having put on the tunic his wife had sent him, came to his slow and agonizing death. He was carried back to Trachis where Deianeira had in the meantime committed suicide on hearing of her catastrophic error. Herakles had himself carried high up on the cliffs of Mount Oeta, and placed on a pyre to be burnt. Beneath him and all around, the world opened out into the far distance: rugged Phtiotis and Thessaly to the north with the valley of the Spercheios in the foreground, Mount Othrys and Pelion to the northeast, Parnassos and the valley of the Kephisos to the south and southeast, and Tymphrestos with the other peaks of the southern Pindos to the west. As the flames flared up from the pyre, suddenly there burst from the rock a stream, the Dyras (Plate 22), in a desperate and vain effort to quench them.[8] The flames burned on and the apotheosis of Herakles took place. But the Dyras is still in this world, a beautifully clear and plentiful stream, nowadays known as the Georgopotamos.

46

CHAPTER

9

THE KEPHISOS OF PHOKIS AND BOEOTIA

The Bellowing Bull

Further yet you went, O far-shooting Apollo, and reached next Cephissus's sweet stream which pours forth its fair-flowing water from Lilaea, and crossing over it, O worker from afar, you passed many-towered Ocalea and reached grassy Haliartus.[1]

OVER THE TRACHIAN mountains a valley opens out to the south, dominated by the mass of towering Parnassos and its neighbouring ridges. Along this valley the main river of Boeotia flows from Phokian territory, deeply embedded in its mythological past, to which poets, mythographers and travellers have not failed to respond.

Some miles down the valley from the north, on its western side, under the buttresses of the Parnassan massif, lies beautiful Lilaia. She was a naiad and a spring, daughter of Kephisos,[2] and she gave her name to the city that sprang up around her, of which some remarkable ruins survive. There, as Homer tells us in the *Iliad*[3] as well as in his Hymn to Apollo, is the source of the Kephisos, over which a priest presided.

There are two springs at Lilaia, from which the river draws its water. The most famous of the two is a fountain within the remains of the city at the foot of its walls. From under the rock bedecked with moss and maidenhair ferns the water wells up clear and icy cold, forming a blue-green pool beneath plane trees. Through an opening it rushes out towards the valley amongst jungly reeds where it joins the water of the other spring. This pours out of the hillside much further up, about a couple of miles away as the crow flies, from where it comes rushing down in little waterfalls shaded by trees (Plate 23).

But it is the fountain down by the city walls that aroused the interest of travellers such as Pausanias, for on the subject of this spring he says: 'It does not always come quietly out of the earth; usually around mid-day it makes a noise as it comes up; you could compare the sound of the water to a bull bellowing'[4].

I spent a whole summer day there and must confess that I heard nothing, at any rate no sound emerging from the spring, not even at noon. But James Frazer remarks that when he went there in the early morning it made 'a gentle mumble', evidently, however, not like the bellowing of a bull. But we should bear in mind that in winter there may be some considerable noise, for Pausanias adds: 'Lilaea is a fine place towards autumn, in summer and spring, but Mount Parnassus does not allow of the water being quite so gentle in winter.'[5] Indeed the neighbouring inhabitants told me that in winter there is a terrific abundance of water pouring out, which must obviously make itself loudly heard. However, it is the song of a nymph one would like to hear at charming Lilaia, as apparently Frazer almost heard, rather than the bellowing of her father's voice. River gods were often in the habit of assuming the form and behaviour of a bull, but spring nymphs never, not even of a cow.

A more fanciful behaviour on the part of the Lilaian spring was how it kept in touch with another spring, according to a story told to Pausanias at Delphi. After stating that Kastalia was supposed, by the poet Panyanis, to be the daughter of Acheloös, he adds that he had heard another account, namely that the water of the spring

> ... was a present to Castalia from the river Cephisus: and this is what Alcaeus says in his prelude to Apollo. It receives strong confirmation from the Lilaeans who drop sweet cakes of their district and other traditional offerings into the spring of the Cephisus on certain special days, and maintain that they come up at Castalia.[6]

I didn't try throwing cakes into the Lilaian fountain; I didn't have any nor did I have time to rush over to Delphi on the other side of Parnassos in order to see whether they reappeared in the water of Kastalia, that other daughter of Kephisos, or was she Acheloös' daughter? River gods had many love affairs and so were in the habit of getting their offspring mixed up, especially where regional rivalries confused the issue.

Among the various human beings Kephisos begat by making love to nymphs and women was Narkissos. Ovid says:

> The dark green nymph Liriope was embraced and ravished by Cephisus in his winding stream, while imprisoned in his waters. When her time came the beauteous nymph

brought forth a child, whom a nymph might love even as a child, and named him Narcissus.[7]

Then there was Eteokles, king of Orchomenos. Hesiod refers to him and to his father Kephisos in connection with the Graces:

> Cephisus is a river at Orchomenus, where also the Graces are worshipped. Eteocles, the son of the river Cephisus, first sacrificed to them. Spouting forth its sweet-flowing water it flows on by Panopeus and through fenced Glechon and through Orchomenus, winding like a snake.[8]

Associated with the Graces the river is also mentioned by Pindar in his fourteenth Olympian Ode: 'Ye that have your portion beside the waters of the Kephisos! Ye that dwell in a home of fair horses! Ye Graces of fertile Orchomenos, ye queens of song that keep watch over the ancient Minyans,[9] listen to my prayer.'

In those days the Kephisos, after passing under the Phocian towns of Davlis and Panopeos and then winding its way eastward, flowed by the ancient Minyan city of Orchomenos and eventually, through a subterranean passage, made its way into the Euboean gulf at Laryma. In addition, at some prehistoric time, the Minyans constructed a number of artificial tunnels, traces of which have been found. Through these the flood waters of Kephisos were drained away. As a result the plain south of Orchomenos was at that time fertile, cultivated land. Subsequently these artificial passages became blocked. According to tradition they were wilfully stopped up by Herakles out of enmity to the Minyans. So the Kopaik lake came into existence. Pausanias tells us:

> The lake at all times covers the greater part of the Orchomonian territory, but in the winter season, after the south-west wind has generally prevailed, the water spreads over a yet greater extent of territory. The Thebans declare that the river Cephisus was diverted into the Orchomenian plain by Herakles and that for a time it passed under the mountain and entered the sea, until Herakles broke up the chasm through the mountain.[10]

The marshy lake, famous for its eels and full of reeds which the ancient Greeks employed for making their wind instruments, subsisted until early in the twentieth century, when the area was reclaimed through drainage works undertaken by an English company.

So it is no longer possible to sail across from 'grassy Hiliartos' to Kopai as Pausanias and other travellers did, and the whole landscape, as described by travellers such as Leake in the nineteenth century, has changed. With its waters much impoverished by irrigation, the Kephisos today flows in an artificial bed through the plain into the Hylikian lake and thence, through another small lake, into the sea. This passage was one of the original outlets.

10

THE BOEOTIAN ASOPOS

A God of Distinguished Progeny

IN THE SOUTH of Boeotia another river of some mythological interest is worth noting. The Asopos, one of the three that bear that name, rises in the slopes of Mount Kithairon near Plataia and flows eastward past Tanagra, along the northern foothills of Parnes, emptying itself into the sea not far from Oropos. Homer refers to the Asopos as a river 'with deep reeds, that couches in the grass'.[1] Indeed it was famous for its reeds,[2] but in consequence of extensive irrigation it flows nowadays much depleted, though still in summer a modest stream, in its ancient bed. Part of its course, far from couching in grass, is stony and rugged.

As a river god, Asopos was of noble birth being the son of Okeanos and Tethys.[3] He had an illustrious history, for amongst other events the battle of Plataia was fought on the river's banks, and distinguished offspring resulted from his love affairs. The Plataians held that Plataia was originally his daughter.[4]

Likewise Antiope was believed by many to be the daughter of Asopos and not of Nykteos;[5] and the Thebans maintained against the Sikyonians that Thebe, who gave her name to the ancient Cadmean city, was the daughter of the Boeotian Asopos, not of the Peloponnesian Asopos.[6] This was the view held by Pindar[7] and Korinna,[8] no doubt for patriotic reasons, both of them being Boeotians, who therefore regarded the story of Asopos and his famous daughters as part of the Boeotian mythological heritage. Accordingly not only Thebe but also Aigina was a daughter of Boeotian Asopos, whom Zeus ravished: 'Beside the waters of the Asopus he once carried off from the portal the deep-breasted maiden, Aegina; then did the golden tresses of the mist hide the overshadowed ridge of the land that so, on the couch immortal',[9] he could lie with her concealed. But I am inclined to favour the Sikyonians who asserted that it was their Asopos whose daughter was ravished by Zeus, a view upheld by Diadorous Siculus and Pausanias. So we shall deal with this myth when we come to the Peloponnese.

11

THE KEPHISOS AND ILISSOS OF ATTICA

THE CONFIGURATION OF Attica, with sweeping lines, articulated limbs and a coast bitingly indented, forms a magnificent landscape to which, however, an extremely low rainfall has been granted. Consequently there are only two rivers of any note and very few lesser streams, though springs are not lacking. Of these two rivers the Kephisos in the summer and the Ilissos throughout most of the year tend to dry up, nowadays more than ever on account of the vast expansion and industrialization of Athens. What is even worse is that much of their respective courses has been covered over and blotted out of sight by urbanization. This is almost totally so in the case of the Ilissos.

Strabo, in his dry style, is none the less clear and to the point in describing these rivers:

> The rivers of Attica are the Cephissus and the Ilissus. The Cephissus has its source in the deme of Trinemeis; it flows through the plain, hence the allusions to the bridge and the 'bridge-jeerings',[1] and then through the legs of the walls which extend from the city to the Peiraeus; it empties itself into the Phaleric Gulf, being a torrential stream most of the time, although in the summer it decreases and entirely gives out. And such is still more the case with the Ilissus, which flows from the other part of the city into the same coast, from the region above Agra and the Lyceium, and from the fountain which is lauded by Plato in the Phaidros.[2]

Being river gods, however, there was a reason, at least as far as the Kephisos was concerned, for running short of water in the summer. Together with Inachos and

Asterion, river gods of Argolis, Kephisos was appointed to act as arbitrator in the dispute between Poseidon and Hera as to which of the two was to be given the region of Argolis. After the three river gods judged in favour of Hera, in a fit of vexation Poseidon withdrew his water from their springs. As a result these rivers are always dry, says Pausanias, unless it rains.[3] Of course there are many Kephisos rivers in Greece, though only two of any importance. There may have been one in Argolis, unidentified as yet and certainly dry. It is perhaps not surprising that the Attic Kephisos, which rises in the foothills of Mount Parnes, is not quite so dry. Some of its springs, in particular the Kephisian one, below Pentelikon, are still running, though perhaps not plentifully enough to keep the river flowing in a dry summer.

In pursuit of this river god through the sprawling suburbs of modern Athens I eventually found him under plane trees, a rather reduced stream bestrewn with discarded plastic bags, but flowing nevertheless in the month of July. It may well be that in the days of Sophocles, several centuries before Strabo and Pausanias, the river, perhaps not yet punished by Poseidon, was plentiful and unpolluted, thus enabling the dramatist to create for us a most evocative picture of the Attic landscape such as it was then, through the chorus welcoming Oedipos as he reached Kolonos, a blind man:

> Stranger, in this land of godly steeds thou hast come to the earth's fairest home, even to our white Colonus, where the nightingale, a constant guest, trills her clear note in the covert of green glades, dwelling amid the wine-dark ivy and the god's inviolate bowers, rich in berries and fruit, unvisited by the sun, unvexed by the wind of any storm, where the reveller Dionysus ever walks the ground, companion of the nymphs that nursed him.
>
> And, fed of heavenly dew, the narcissus blooms morn by morn with fair clusters, crown of the two Great Goddesses from of yore; and the crocus blooms with golden beam. Nor fail the sleepless founts whence the waters of the Cephisus water, but each day with stainless tide he moveth over the plains of the land's swelling busom, for the giving of quick increase, nor hath the Muses's quire disdained this place, nor Aphrodite of the golden rein.[4]

Kephisos, as a river god, was greatly revered. He received locks of hair from youths as offerings[5] and, for instance, a whole section of an altar was dedicated to him and to Acheloös in the temple of Amphiaraos at Oropos.[6] Moreover his progeny played an important part in mythology, for Prokris, whose story with Kephalos has been so charmingly related by Ovid,[7] and Oreithyia, who was carried off by Boreas, the north wind, whilst playing and dancing on the banks of the Ilissos, were his granddaughters.[8]

But the most remarkable feature of Kephisos is that he as well as Ilissos was represented in sculpture. Euripides calls him 'bull-visaged',[9] which is not at all surprising since river gods were often represented with a bull's head on coins, though on the Parthenon he was not given that aspect. We do not find many river gods in the Greek sculpture that has come down to us. However both Kephisos and Ilissos, represented in human form by the sculptors of the Parthenon, have survived. Kephisos appears as a magnificent male body reclining in the left corner of the west pediment and is now in the British Museum (Plate 24). The Ilissos, in the opposite corner, is likewise personified by a male figure, now in the Acropolis museum.[10] And again, on a charming fifth-century BC Attic relief in the National Museum of Athens,[11] Kephisos is represented as a bearded man leading three nymphs before Hermes.

Besides Kephisos and Ilissos I know of only two other Greek river gods represented in sculpture that have survived: Alpheios and Kladeos on the west pediment of the temple to Zeus at Olympia. But of course other river gods in sculpture did exist, for instance Erymanthos in a shrine at Psophis dedicated to him and mentioned by Pausanias.[12]

The Ilissos, which comes down from various springs on the Hymettos slopes, has fared even more sadly than the Kephisos as the result of urbanization, for it doesn't flow at all and fails to reach the Kephisos, which it should be doing. Its course is practically invisible nowadays. But in ancient time the Ilissos no doubt flowed most idyllically, so that in its landscape the tale of Prokris and Kephalos, and of Oreithyia and Boreas could come into being and inspire poets. One of its main springs is now an enchanting fountain in the wall of the Keseriani monastery and here, or in its neighbourhood, it is possible, with a little imagination and the help of Plato's *Phaidros* in our hands, to figure out to ourselves what the stream must have been like in those days:

Phaidros: … Where shall we sit and read?

Socrates: Let us turn aside here and go along the Illissus; then we can sit down quietly wherever we please.

Phaidros: I am fortunate, it seems, being barefoot; you are so always. It is easiest then for us to go along the brook with our feet in the water, and it is not unpleasant, especially at this time of the year and the day.

Socrates: Lead on, and look for a good place where we may sit.

Phaidros: Do you see that very tall plane tree?

Socrates: What of it?

Phaidros: There is shade there and a moderate breeze and grass to sit on, or, if we like, to lie down on.

Socrates: Lead the way.

Phaidros: Tell me, Socrates, is it from some place along here by the Ilissos that Boreas is said to have carried off Oreithyia?

Socrates: Yes, that is the story.

Phaidros: Well, is it from here? The stream looks very pretty and pure and clear and fit for girls to play by.

Socrates: No, the place is about two or three furlongs further down, where you cross over to the precinct of Agra; and there is an altar of Boreas somewhere thereabouts.

Phaidros: I have never noticed it. But, for Zeus's sake, Socrates tell me: Do you believe this tale is true?

21 The Spercheios, rising in the mountains of western Greece and flowing east into the Euboean Gulf, was the river god whom Achilles loved so intensely that, in the custom of the times, he cut off one of his beautiful locks and donated it to Spercheios.

22 The Dyras, known today as the Georgopotamos, was revered as the river god which burst forth from the earth in a desperate but vain attempt to quench the funeral pyre on which Herakles was determined to die following the suicide of his jealous wife Deianeira.

23 One of the springs of the Lilaia is the source of the Boeotian Kephisos. Lilaia was a Naiad and daughter of the river god Kephisos.

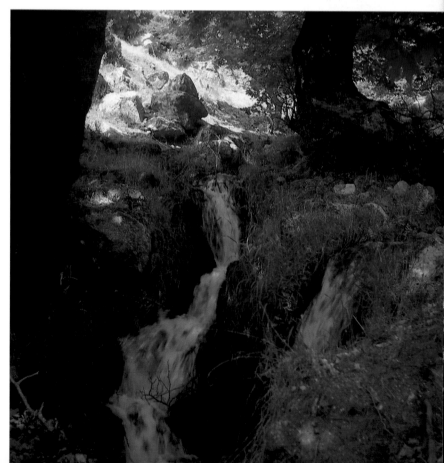

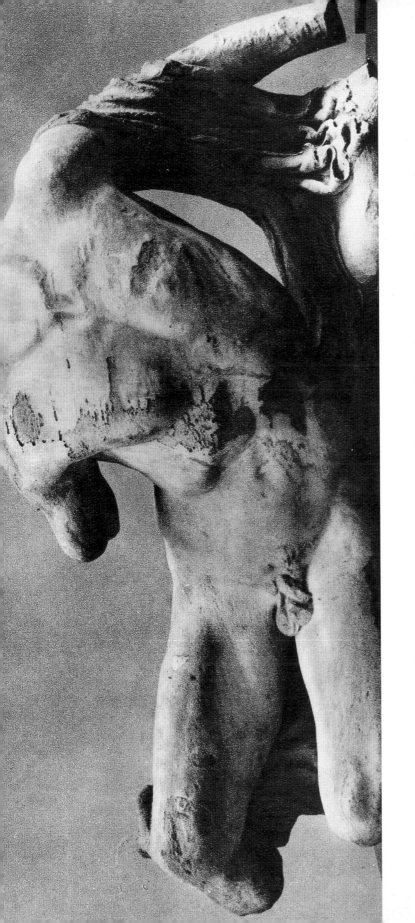

24 Kephisos of Attica, like other river gods, often assumed the form of a bull. But in this depiction on the west pediment of the Parthenon, this much revered river god of Attica is represented in human form. The river is not abundant in water because, in a fit of pique over a dispute, Poseidon punished Kephisos by withholding his waters from the river god.

25 The Asopos in the Peloponnese represents the river god whose daughter Aigina was carried off by Zeus. When Asopos pursued him Zeus hurled thunderbolts at the aggrieved father. Coal and volcanic deposits in the river may have fed this ancient myth, but no traces of such deposits have been found in modern times.

26 The terrible Styx, high up in the mountains of Arcadia, was dreaded by the Olympian gods, for if any of them, according to Hesiod, broke an oath he had taken by her he would have to suffer ghastly punishment of long duration.

Socrates: If I disbelieved, as the wise men do, I should not be extraordinary; then I might give a rational explanation. ... But I have no leisure for them all; and the reason, my friend, is this: I am not yet able, as the Delphic inscription has it, to know myself; so it seems to me ridiculous, when I do not yet know that, to investigate irrelevant things. And so I dismiss the matter and accepting the customary belief about them I investigate not these things but myself. ... But, my friend, while we were talking, is not this the tree to which you were leading us?

Phaidros: Yes, this is it.

Socrates: By Hera, it is a charming resting place. For this plane tree is very spreading and lofty, and the tall and shady willow is very beautiful, and it is full of bloom, so as to make the place most fragrant; then, too, the spring is very pretty as it flows under the plane tree, and its water is very cool, to judge by my foot. And it seems to me a sacred place of some nymphs and the Achelous, judging by the figurines and statues. Then again, if you please, how lovely and perfectly charming the breeziness of the place is! And it resounds with the shrill summer music of the chorus of the cicadas. But the most delightful thing of all is the grass, as it grows on the gentle slope, thick enough to be just right when you lay your head on it. So you have guided the stranger most excellently, dear Phaidros. ... So now that I have come here, I intend to lie down, and do you choose the position in which you think you can read most easily, and read.[13]

Whether this famous walk and talk took place in such a form and exactly in such terms, or whether Plato's own descriptive talent, sense of observation, imagination and gift of characterization re-created the picture from the kernel of something he knew had happened, no matter. The picture of the whole scene is more evocative, more idyllic, more convincingly true to life than anything in the whole pastoral literature of ancient Greece and Rome because of its localization, its immediacy, because it consists of a faithful description of the Ilissos such as it then was and such as it could be enjoyed by anyone responsive to the beauties of nature. If practically all traces of this stream have been swept away by our modern trend of civilization, we can console ourselves that there still are streams in Greece which, though under constant threat, retain much of that character the Ilissos once had – the purling spring that feeds it, the cool and clear water rushing by, the grass shaded by the overhanging plane tree, the cicadas dizzily chirping in the heat of the summer day.

PART

THE
PELOPONNESE

THE RIVER GODS of the Peloponnese may be considered in three groups.

The River Gods of Argolis

The scenery of Argolis has an ascetic, translucent quality and a bone structure most delicately, though sparingly, covered with vegetation, so that the main limbs are distinctly visible as they surge and sink into protean distances of ethereal colouring. If there are other parts of Greece that appear dry to the traveller, Argolis will strike him as even drier. 'Thirsty Argos', says Homer.[1] And yet there are fertile stretches, such as the plain of Argos itself, green with intense citrus cultivation. Indeed Strabo argues that Argos is very far from being waterless.[2] But practically all its rivers are dry in the summer, or if they still flow in their upper reaches their water is soon drained away for irrigation. Nevertheless at least three rivers of Argolis are mythologically important – the Inachos, the Erasinas and the Hyllikos – they were river gods. I will discuss them in Chapters 12, 13 and 14.

Achaia and Corinthia

Pines high up on the beetling promontories and chalky cliffs, cypresses and citrus trees on the low-lying stretch of land, orchards, rocks and shingle beaches by the sea, with lordly Parnassos looming from across the gulf – these are the distinctive features of the northern coast of the Peloponnese. Achaia and Corinthia – a strip of land between the mountains and the sea, deeply furrowed by ravines and gullies in which rivers flow, but in most cases fail to reach the sea in the dryer months of the year. This is again partly the result of irrigation and cultivation, though not entirely so, for most of these streams are real torrents. They played a minor part in mythology, except for the Asopos, discussed in Chapter 16, a real river and a prominent river god in ancient times.

Of these lesser streams or torrents the Selemnos, the Bolinaios, the Selinos, the Boura and the Krathis (see Chapter 15) are worth taking into account only because some of their mythological or historical aspects have been recorded, though it cannot be said that they were prominent river gods. We know practically nothing about them as such.

The River Gods of Arcadia, Elis, Lakonia and Messenia

In that mass of rugged territory formed by the uplands of Arcadia, nearly all the major Peloponnesian rivers rise, flowing eastward and southward into the adjacent regions. They are the subject of Chapter 17 and all subsequent chapters of this book. Very few of them run dry even in the summer. Some of the most magnificent scenery of Greece is to be found here, where cliffs, gorges and woods affect the character of the rivers most incisively.

Of the Peloponnesian regions, Arcadia was the richest not only in springs but also in myths. Its people were somewhat backward compared with those of other parts of Greece. They were rude shepherds and hardy mercenaries, speaking a pre-Doric Greek and leading a pastoral life far removed from the Theocritan world in which they were supposed by late writers to bask. But they must have been gifted with exceptional imagination. They gave rise to a wealth of myths which spread all over Greece, leaving their imprint on the rivers of those regions and providing wonderful material for poets and mythographers.

12

THE INACHOS
Punished by Poseidon

DRY THOUGH IT is for most of the year round, the Inachos is the principal river of Argolis, and indeed we know why it is so dry, at any rate if we accept the explanation of mythology. In accordance with an ancient line of tradition, Pausanias says this:

> Phoroneus was the first inhabitant of the land and Inachus, the father of Phoroneus, was not a man but a river. This river, with the rivers of Cephisus and Asterion,[1] judged concerning the land between Poseidon and Hera. They decided that the land belonged to Hera, and so Poseidon made their waters disappear. For this reason neither the Inachus nor either of the other rivers I have mentioned provides any water except after rain.[2]

Further on in his account Pausanias adds: 'Above Oenoë is Mount Artemesius, with a sanctuary of Artemis on the top. On this mountain are also the springs of the river Inachus. For it really has springs, though the water makes little progress across the country.'[3] The valley in which the river course lies is not lacking in vegetation, however, nor in natural beauty for that matter, the cypress tree being a conspicuous feature of its articulate landscape.

In referring to the same story of Poseidon's punishment and the resultant dryness of the country, Apollodoros tells us that Danaos, king of Argos, sent his daughters to draw water:

> One of them, Amymone, in her search for water threw a dart at a deer and hit a sleeping satyr, and he, starting up, desired to force her; but Poseidon appearing on the scene, the satyr fled, and Anymone lay with Poseidon, and he revealed to her the springs of Lerna.[4]

Evidently Poseidon was preferable to lie with, rather than a satyr, all the more so since he was able to reward Amymone by turning her into a river, so one gathers by inference. Pity Ovid missed this story out. So delighted was the god that he struck the ground with his trident and up welled some springs from the ground, which is why Euripides in his *Phoinissai* refers to 'Lerna's Trident and the waters of Amymone, dear to Poseidon'.[5] These springs, situated a few miles south of Argos, are of course famous for the Hydra which had its lair there and which Herakles killed in his second labour. The Lernian springs, which flow perennially, are close to the sea and do not give rise to a river. As for the river Amymone, mentioned by Pausanias,[6] next to whose spring the plane tree grew under which the Hydra was reared, its waters have been drained away by irrigation like those of many other streams.

We find the river god Inachos, son of Okeanos and Tethys,[7] already mentioned by Hesiod, or the contemporary writer of the Great Eoiai, who says that Mycenae was the river's daughter and that from her the city received its name.[8] We find Aeschylus referring to the river god Inachos as the recipient of offerings and sacrifices. Orestes cuts off two locks of his hair for him: 'A lock to Inachus in requital of my nurture; and here a second in token of my grief.'[9] And then, with reference to the pathetic story of Io, who was ravished by Zeus and subsequently turned, by jealous Hera, into a heifer eternally pursued by a stinging gadfly, Aeschylus mentions the river god again, in this context as a father. Prometheus exclaims: 'How can I fail to hear the maiden frenzied by the gadfly, the daughter of Inachus? She it is who fires the heart of Zeus with passion, and now, through Hera's fate, is disciplined perforce by wandering eternally.'[10]

The divinity of the river persisted in the minds, cult and writings of people for very many centuries. Deeply woven in the mythology of the country, the Inachos surfaces again with Ovid, evidently a little more plentifully supplied with water than it usually is. Ovid tells us that only Inachos, on account of his own grief, failed to come to console Peneios for the fate of his daughter Daphne, metamorphosed into a laurel tree:

> Hidden away in his deepest cave, he augments his waters with his tears, and in utmost wretchedness laments his daughter, Io, as lost. He knows not whether she still lives or is among the shades. But, since he cannot find her anywhere, he thinks she must be nowhere, and his anxious soul forbodes things worse than death.[11]

So we find the whole valley of the Inachos and the ancient plain of Argos, through which the torrent digs its course, replete with a mythological past whose ramifications stretch out in all directions.

CHAPTER

13

THE ERASINOS
A Vanished River God

A few miles south of Argos there flowed once upon a time a river that was a river god – the Erasinos. Although its course was short, its waters, which reached the sea, were abundant. Nowadays the river has disappeared, the water being totally absorbed by irrigation. But the spring itself is as plentiful as ever. Dodwell, who travelled there at the beginning of the nineteenth century, described it as follows:

> In fifty minutes from Argo we reached a cave in the rock, which contains a church, and a spring of clear water, called Kephalari, which bursts from the rock with impetuosity. This is the Erasinus which, according to Herodotus, Strabo and Pausanias, has its original source at the lake Stymphalus in Arcadia. After a subterranean course of about 200 stadia it issues from this cavern, which is in Mount Chaon. Bacchus and Pan here received the sacrifices of the devout. The rock has been cut and the cave was probably a Paneion, or nymphaion.[1]

The church is still there but has been renovated since Dodwell's day, and much of the site is now occupied by restaurants and a recreation pine grove littered with plastic rubbish, so that the numinous character of the site has virtually vanished. Nevertheless the gushing spring, its rock and surrounding plane trees create an impressive picture which still reflects, though dimly, a place where Bakhos and Pan were once venerated.

Herodotus, after stating that, according to reports, there is a pitch-dark chasm at Stymphalos, into which the waters of the lake empty themselves to reappear near Argos where they give rise to the Erasinos, adds the following:

> Cleomenes, having arrived on the banks of the river, proceeded to offer sacrifices to it,

but in spite of all that he could do, the victims were not favourable to his crossing. So he said that he admired the god for refusing to betray his countrymen, but still the Argives should not escape from him for all that.[2]

Evidently Erasinos was a powerful river god with a will of his own, and his stream, in those days, must have been a substantial one.

Strabo repeats more or less what Herodotus says about the Stymphalian source of the Erasinos;[3] Pausanias says that the Erasinos falls into the Phryxios which flows into the sea.[4] This statement is confusing and probably inaccurate. In any case irrigation has left no trace of either. But in referring to the source of the Erasinos at Stymphalos, Pausanias gives us an interesting account of what the lake was like in his day, evidently much smaller than it is at present.[5]

Since underground passages for watercourses are frequent in Greece, it is not at all improbable that the Kephalari spring should draw its water from the Stymphalian lake. The connection between the two is supported by modern topographers and geologists.[6] A similar situation, for instance, is to be found in Arcadia with regard to the source of the Eurotas and Lake Takka, and again in Epiros between the Thyamis and the Ioannina lake.

CHAPTER

14

THE HYLLIKOS AND THE GOLDEN STREAM THAT NEVER DIES

IN ONE OF the most beautiful corners of Argolis, facing the island of Poros, the promontory of Methana and the Saronic gulf, are situated the remains of Troizen, where an atmosphere survives full of stories about Theseus, Phaidra and Hippolitos. Pausanias has left us a detailed description of the ancient city, its surroundings, monuments and vestiges such as they then were.[1] Amongst other things he says:

> There is a sanctuary of Zeus Saviour which they say was the work of King Aetios, and there is water they call the Golden Stream; there was a drought of nine years in which the god never rained, when, they say, all their other watersprings dried up, but the Golden Stream kept on flowing the same as ever.

The spring is most probably the one that is situated a couple of miles from the village of Damala, now misleadingly renamed Troizen, on the left bank of a stream at a point where the gorge, in which it flows, opens out into the plain. The spring gushes down onto a ledge in the hillside shaded by plane trees, about forty or fifty feet above the level of the river, into which it then steeply pours. There is a stone bridge in one single piece leading over the stream a few yards away from the spring, known as the Devil's Bridge,[2] which used to be an aquaduct. There are here no traces of a sanctuary, if by ἱερὸν Pausanias meant a stone structure and not just a holy place; but a few paces from the spring and forming part of the site are several small niches carved in the porous face of the overhanging rock, which must once have contained figurines and offerings. So there can be no doubt that it was a place of worship. One is inclined to feel, in the *religio loci*, that such worship was directed to the local nymphs and to Pan, rather than to Zeus Saviour. Indeed, the stone of the former aquaduct bears the imprint of a cloven foot, hence the name Devil's Bridge, so the village people say. But I cannot help feeling that if a live cloven foot ever left this imprint, it was Pan's rather than the Devil's, for the place is saturated with an atmosphere of Pan far removed from the world of the Christian Devil. With the coming of Christianity, however, Pan was probably turned into the Devil in order to stamp out pagan worship from those haunts where nymphs presided.

The river into which the Golden Stream pours is in all probability the Hyllikos whose source, mentioned by Pausanias,[3] is up the valley close to the ridge that separates Trizenia from Hermione to the southwest.

The Hyllikos is a modest stream, not a great river, but it never runs dry (hence the name 'Golden Stream'), though in summer its water fails to reach the sea, again on account of irrigation and farming. At the opening of the gorge there are tanks in which the water is collected and stored, and from which it is then directed through pipes into the fields of the narrow plain that stretches from the mountains to the sea. But in the gorge, where the water perennially flows, the Hyllikos is one of the most enchanting streams of Greece, for it has limestone boulders brilliantly white, carved into a variety of shapes by the current and pools under plane trees enshrined in oleander and festooned with creepers and ferns. One situation after another is created in which our senses delight.

No records in writing of the Hyllikos as a river god have survived, but the traces of worship on its banks and the numinous atmosphere in its gorge betoken ancient divinity.

15

THE SELEMNOS AND OTHER LESSER STREAMS OF THE NORTHERN PELOPONNESE

IF WE PROCEED eastward from Patras along the coast, as Pausanias did, shortly before the Drepanon promontory we come to a dry torrent, virtually obliterated nowadays. Pausanias calls it a river, and in his days it may well have been somewhat more like a river. He says:

> The local people have a legend about it, they say Selemnus was a beautiful shepherd lad working here, and Argyra was one of the nymphs in the sea; she fell in love with Selemnus, and they say she used to come up out of the sea to visit him and to sleep with him. But it was not long before Selemnus no longer looked so beautiful and the nymph would not visit him any more, and so Selemnus lost his Argyra and died of love, and Aphrodite turned him into a river. I am telling you the story told at Patrae. Even as water he still loved Argyra, just as Alpheius in the legend still loves Arethusa; so Aphrodite gave Selemnus another favour, and now the river has forgotten Argyra. I did hear another legend about him, that the water of Selemnus is equally good for a man or a woman, to cure the wounds of love, and if you wash in the river you forget your passion. If there is any truth in this legend, the water of Selemnus is worth more to mankind than a good deal of money.[1]

Bolinaios and the Selinos

At a short distance beyond the Selemnos as you travel along the coast there is another torrent, the Bolinaios, which comes down Mount Panachaikon pathetically dry throughout most of year and disfigured by the motorway bridge and other constructions. No doubt it was more attractive in the past; it is worth mentioning because Pausanias reports as follows: 'They say Apollo fell in love with a young virgin called Boline and she ran away and threw herself into the sea here, and the favour of Apollo made her immortal.'[2]

The Selinos, which flows a few miles beyond Aigion into the sea and is often dry, is only worth mentioning in relation to Helike, a city which stood close by, famous for its sanctuary of Poseidon and several times referred to by Homer. But Poseidon's suppliants having been forcefully pulled out of the sanctuary, Helike was destroyed in 373 BC by an earthquake which the god brought about as punishment.[3]

The Boura and the Krathis: One Famous for Its Cave, the Other for Its Water from the Styx

The Boura comes down to the sea in an impressive gorge with very little water, if any at all, though in its Arcadian upper reaches it flows more plentifully.

It was famous for a grotto in a cliff of its gorge in which stood a sacred statue of Herakles. Pausanias says that it gave oracles with a board of dice.[4] The cave was often visited by travellers in the nineteenth century, when it was still full of niches and votive offerings, but has now vanished as the result of earthquakes.

The Krathis a few miles further east,[5] which likewise rises in the Arcadian mountains, is plentifully supplied with water, one of its main sources, or tributaries, being the fabulous Styx. Indeed Herodotus refers to the Krathis as 'a stream which is never dry',[6] no doubt because most of the other rivers of the coast ran out of water then as they do now. But mythology is reticent on the subject of both the Krathis and the Boura.

CHAPTER

16

THE ASOPOS OF PHLEIUS

Sent Home with Thunderbolts

THE ASOPOS OF Phleius and Sikyonia is a river deeply embedded in mythology, a river with numerous as well as celebrated offspring, sons and daughters, one of whom was to prove a source of great affliction to him. Apollodoros tells us:

> The Asopus river was a son of Oceanus and Tethys, or, as Acusilaus[1] says, of Pero and Poseidon, or, according to some, of Zeus and Eurynome. Him Metope, herself a daughter of the river Ladon, married and bore two sons, Ismenas and Pelagon, and twenty daughters, one of whom, Aegina, was carried off by Zeus. Asopus came to Corinth in search of her, and learnt from Sisyphus that the ravisher was Zeus. Asopus pursued him, but Zeus by hurling thunderbolts, sent him away back to his own streams; hence coals are fetched to this day from the streams of that river. And having conveyed Aegina to the island then named Oenone, but now called Aegina after her, Zeus cohabited with her and begat a son Aeacus, on her.[2]

It may well be that at one time the Asopos had coal deposits and volcanic outbursts of which there are, however, no traces today. Statius, in his florid verse, refers to the 'brave river blowing ashes of thunderbolts and Aetnaean vapours from its panting banks to the sky'.[3] Poor Asopos, Sisyphos's disclosure didn't help him in the least, whilst the punishment Sisyphos suffered in Hades for having turned informer seems somewhat excessive. But apparently he was guilty of other offences.

Pausanias enlarges on the subject with further information:

On the summit of Acrocorinth is a temple of Aphrodite. The images are of Aphrodite armed, Helius and Eros with a bow. The spring, which is behind the temple, they say was the gift of Asopus to Sisyphus. The latter knew, so runs the legend, that Zeus had ravished Aegina, the daughter of Asopus, but refused to give information to the seeker before he had a spring given to him on Acrocorinth. When Asopus granted this request, Sisyphus turned informer, and on this account he receives – if anyone believes the story – punishment in Hades. I have heard people say that this spring and Peirene are the same, the water in the city flowing hence underground.

The Asopus rises in Phliasian territory, flows through Sicyonian, and empties itself into the sea there. His daughters, say the Phliasians, were Corcyra, Aegina and Thebe. Corcyra and Aegina gave new names to the islands of Scheria and Oenone, while from Thebe is named the city below Cadmea. The Thebans do not agree, but say that Thebe was the daughter of the Boeotian, not the Phliasian, Asopus.[4]

So of course Pindar in his eighth Isthmian Ode is patriotically referring to the Boeotian river as the father of Aegina and Thebe. But Diadoros Siculus is in agreement with Apollodoros and Pausanias, for he maintains that the father of Aigina was the Phliasian river.[5] And Bakchylides, in his Thirty-sixth Song for Automedes of Phleius, victor in the pentathlon contest at Nemea, is definitely referring to the Peloponnesian river when he extols the river god's fame and that of his daughters including Thebe and Aigina, whom he mentions by name. It is perhaps worth adding that the children of Asopos' great-grandson Phokos, settled in Phokis and gave their father's name to that part of Greece.[6]

The Asopos flows without turning dry throughout the year in the territory that lies between Nemea and Sikyon, a leafy, gentle stream with willows, poplars, plane trees and reeds along its banks (Plate 25), its course running northeastward through a deep, green valley with steep hills on either side. The source is in the Stymphalian lake from which the river draws its water through a subterranean passage, far shorter, however, than the underground watercourse of the Erasinos, the existence of which, if not certain, seems likely.

So then this reedy lake, situated in magnificent surroundings, dominated by Mount Kyllene and lofty Arcadian ridges, and celebrated for its savage birds which Herakles on his sixth labour chased away with a brazen rattle, gives rise to two rivers that were revered as deities.

CHAPTER

17

THE STYX
The Terrible Goddess

And there dwells the goddess loathed by the deathless gods, terrible Styx, eldest daughter of backflowing Oceanus. She lives apart from the gods in her glorious house vaulted over with great rocks and propped up to heaven all around with silver pillars. Rarely does the daughter of Thaumas, swift-footed Iris, come to her with a message over the sea's wide back. But when strife and quarrel arise among the deathless gods, and when any one of them who live in the house of Olympus lies, then Zeus sends Iris to bring in a golden jug the great oath of the gods from far away, the famous cold water which trickles down from the high and beetling rocks. ... For whoever of the deathless gods that hold the peaks of snowy Olympus pours a libation of her water and is forsworn, lies breathless until a full year is completed, and never comes near to taste ambrosia and nectar, but lies spiritless and voiceless on a strewn bed: and a heavy trance overshadows him. But when he has spent a long year in his sickness, another penance and a harder follows after the first. For nine years he is cut off from the eternal gods and never joins their councils or their feasts, nine full years. But in the tenth year he comes again to join the assemblies of the deathless gods who live in the house of Olympus. Such an oath then did the gods appoint the eternal and primaeval water of the Styx to be: and it spouts through a rugged place.[1]

HIGH UP ON the edge of the great limestone face of Mount Aroanios there it is, this primeval water spouting straight into the space of a precipice six hundred feet deep. You can see it today as Hesiod described it more than two and a half millennia ago – one of the grandest sights of Greece, difficult to reach, so rugged, rocky and sheer is the access. Through dark conifer forests from the rushing Krathis river you climb into this luminous stronghold of Arcadia. Mount Aroanios, the Chelmos of our times, its summit nearing eight thousand feet, towers above you as you approach its sheer cliffs yellow, pink and mauve in colour, with patches of snow still clinging to the rock in the height of summer (Plate 26). As the water of the Styx – Στύγος ὕδωρ – comes over the rim of the mountain crown from the snows that collect and then melt in the sun, it is wafted by the wind into a great leap, often becoming a spray so thin in the air that you can hardly see it. Being at times blown against the perpendicular side of the cliff, it has left in the rock a dark, almost black scar visible from afar. This accounts for the name Mavroneri by which the Styx is known to the shepherds and inhabitants of the neighbouring villages – Black Water. But it is limpid clear, as well as icy cold, and not at all lethal as it was believed to be in ancient times.

Pausanias, who approached it from the interior of Arcadia, describes the area as follows:

As you go from Pheneus to the west, the left road leads to Cleitor, while on the right is the road to Nonacris and the water of the Styx. Of old, Nonacris was a town of the Arcadians that was named after the wife of Lycaon. When I visited it, it was in ruins, and many of these were scarcely to be seen. Not far from the ruins is a high cliff; I know of none other that rises to so great a height. A stream drops down the cliff, called by the Greeks the water of the Styx.

Hesiod in the Theogony[2] ... speaks of Styx as the daughter of Oceanus and the wife of Palla. ... But it is Homer who introduces most frequently the name of Styx into poetry. In the oath of Hera he writes:

'Witness now to this be Earth, and broad Heaven above,
And the water of Styx down-flowing.'

These verses suggest that the poet had seen the water of the Styx dripping down ...

The stream spouting down the cliff by the side of Nonacris falls first to a high rock, through which it passes and then descends into the river Crathis. Its water brings death to all, man and beast alike.[3]

After this realistic picture of the actual site Pausanias goes on to describe the fabulous properties of the water which was said to dissolve glass, stone, pottery and even gold.

No traces of Nonakris have survived, which is not surprising since Pausanias says there were hardly any ruins visible in his own day. So its exact location has not yet been discovered, but it cannot have been far from the present village of Solos which lies near the confluence of the Krathis with the stream formed by the Styx after falling from its cliff. Herodotus makes a curious statement about Nonakris and the Styx.[4] Referring to Kleomenes and his machinations in Arcadia to muster support against Sparta – events that took place six hundred years before the days of Pausanias when Nonakris was flourishing – he says that in that city the Styx consisted of a little water dripping from a rock into a basin. This may have been a fountain to which the water was conveyed from the stream of the Styx after its drop, but it is obvious that Herodotus had never visited the place.

27 Lousios, literally the Wash, is the river god of the Peloponnese, in whose waters the infant Zeus was washed according to local tradition.

28 The river Lousios in places pours abundantly from rock to rock and, in places such as here, more majestically from pool to pool – a worthy site in which to bathe the infant god of gods.

29 The Ladon, here seen at its source, is a river rich in myths. In some versions of the mythical tales Ladon, not Peneios, was the river god father of Daphne. In these sources Daphne, again anxious to safeguard her virginity, stabs to death her companion, whom she discovers to be a male suitor disguised as a young female come to bathe with her in the Ladon.

30 At the confluence of the Ladon and the Erymanthos, both river gods of the Peloponnese, the mighty waters of the Ladon appear to dominate the more gentle stream of the Erymanthos.

31 The Erymanthos, with its surrounding wooded heights, was where the centaurs took refuge after having been expelled from Mount Pelion by the Lapiths.

There can be no doubt that the ancient Greeks regarded the Styx as a stream of clear water falling from a lofty, precipitous crag. In his numerous references to the Styx,[5] Homer repeatedly describes it as 'sheer-falling' or 'down-falling' water. It was only later poets and mythographers, particularly Latin poets, who envisaged it not as a down-falling stream or waterfall, but as a river in Hades or a lake, far from limpid-clear. By the time it reached Dante in the *Inferno*, via Virgil's Stygian marsh, it had become a muddy swamp:

> L'acqua era buia molto più che persa;
> E noi in compagnia dell'onde bige
> Entrammo giù per una via diversa.
>
> Una palude fa, ch'a nome Stige,
> Questo tristo ruscel, quando è disceso
> Al piè delle maligne piagge grige.
>
> E io che di mirar mi stava inteso
> Vidi gente fangose in quel pantano
> Ignude tutte, e con sembiante offeso.[6]

The image of a clear, though icy cold and deadly poisonous stream, pouring down from a beetling cliff lit up by the blue sky of Greece, and of Iris speeding across the air from Mount Olympus to Mount Aroanios holding a golden jug to be filled with oath-binding water, thus faded away in the course of centuries and was replaced by that of a muddy swamp in hell. It may be that Homer himself was partly responsible for the gradual change, since in two of his many passages referring to the Styx he places it in Hades;[7] but he always retains, none the less, and stresses, the proper character of the site, namely that of a towering rock from which the stream pours down. Hesiod associates the Styx with Hades, but in a loose manner, emphasizing that the goddess lived apart, in her rocky house propped up to Heaven – Πρὸς οὐρανὸν – all round with silver pillars.

Of course, far more responsible for the distortion was Plato, who in his fanciful description of Hades appears to be the first to envisage the Styx as a lake,[8] though it was the imagination of others that made it swampy and muddy.

Herodotus and Strabo both confirm that the Styx was geographically situated high up in Arcadia.[9]

18

THE AROANIOS AND ITS SPRINGS

Where the Trout Sang

IN A VALLEY on the southern side of Mount Aroanios, a stream flows for a couple of miles before reaching the Aroanios river of which, though a tributary, it is the main source. It gushes abundantly and unexpectedly out of the rocky face of a cliff, welling up at the same time close by, from the ground, through pebbles and moss, where great plane trees congregate. The site is known locally as Pegai, or the Springs, and there are said to be seven of these. Their waters, after rushing forward in various gullies or brooks, gather together a few hundred yards further down the valley, followed by a leafy grove of plane trees which shade their banks covered with ferns and moss. The stream is full of trout. Pausanias, who visited the site, describes them as follows:

> Among the fish of the Aroanios is one called the dappled fish. These dappled fish, it is said, utter a cry like that of a thrush. I have seen fish that have been caught, but never heard their cry, though I watched by the river even until sunset, at which time the fish were said to cry most.[1]

Pausanias was unlucky.

Thirty years ago I described this stream and its springs in a short story from which I here quote not the most relevant passage where it is related how the trout were indeed heard to sing, but one that provides a picture of the site as it then was and as seen by an approaching traveller:

> The valley grew narrower; the fields of Indian corn, hemmed in between the cliffs,

hugged closer to the poplars and then dwindled out for lack of level ground. Now all was rugged and wild. We crossed over pebbles and stones where the main bed of the river became dry. The waters were rushing down from the right through a narrow ravine. In this direction we followed the path upstream which was shaded by the thick foliage of oriental plane trees. The insistent zigzag screeching of the cicadas which had deafened us into a state of torpor earlier in the day subsided, soothed and drowned by the roar of the rushing waters. Then suddenly the plane trees parted and we entered a glade with a mill across the stream and a tiny coffee house on our side of the banks. At this point the stream divided into various ramifications. Above the old mill and plane trees Aroanios, now known as Mount Chelmos, rose sheer in a sublime cone of limestone nearly eight thousand feet high, shimmering pink and gold in the evening light.

There are moments and places in our lives where nature, as if to amuse herself, contrives to place before us a combination of elements brought together in such a way as to strike deep into our senses and make us gasp. Such was my encounter with Pegais. ...

I followed the winding channels of water upstream under the plane trees, which from time to time parted to let through the towering shape of Aroanios like a Titan in search of a nymph, a giant turned to stone by the jealousy of a god. Within a quarter of a mile a red cliff rose sheer, at the foot of which the stream started, and within a radius of about one hundred yards I found seven springs bubbling up from the ground or out of the rock.

They rippled down over stones and moss, feeding the various branches of the stream with the clearest and coldest water I had ever come across. I started to explore each branch from its source, following it downhill toward the mill where they all converged, like a delta in reverse. Their banks were fringed with hollyhock, morning glory, and wild daisies in bloom, and overhung with twisted branches of plane. A strip of ground separated every stream from the other, earth, gravel and moss, varying in width from about five yards to fifty, and here and there on these banks shaded by the trees, wherever the ground was level, the shepherds would gather with their flocks at noon, calling out and piping their tunes before their midday siesta.

In my exploration I proceeded to cross from one bank to the other. I found that I could sometimes jump across the stream, usually three or four yards wide, by stepping on a large stone and leaping to the next one. But often I found myself having to wade through knee-deep with the icy current whirling round my legs. Though the temperature and rush of water felt like a whip on the bare skin, lashing me across, the sensation was bracing.

On my second day at Pegai I discovered my favourite stream. It was the far-end one from the mill, the seventh, fed by the seventh spring farther up, where it purled out of the rock over stones and moss, a glitter of diamonds turning liquid.[2]

This was many years ago and much has changed since then. The mill, now in decay, is no longer used. A tarmac road has been built and cars crowd the site where a trout market has been established with sheds and stalls for the sale of fish which are bred in an artificial pond. Much of the spring's water is drained away and the plentiful rills of the past are dry. The ground is littered with plastic bags and rubbish. Pegai is unrecognizable today.

73

19

THE LADON
Rich in Offspring and in Stories

WITH MANY FACETS and features, as well as many shadows clinging to its banks out of the remote past, the Ladon winds its way from the uplands of Arcadia into the Alpheian waters of luxuriantly green Elis, a tributary that figures prominently among the fluvial deities of the Peloponnese. Pausanias regarded it as the most beautiful river in Greece,[1] an exaggerated assessment perhaps. But there where it rises, the atmosphere of its mythical life still haunts the water, the banks and the trees that overhang the spring (Plate 29). I quote again from the same short story already referred to:

> It rises fully fledged from the bowels of the earth like a sudden gift of the gods. A deep pool, serpentine in colour, collects at the foot of a perpendicular cliff. Its uncanny waters, encircled by willows and plane trees, are held still without a ripple as under the spell of a wizard. But they are motionless only in appearance, for through an outlet a few yards in width they pour swiftly over stones and logs of wood into a bed which winds its way down, at first through a gentle landscape and then into a majestic gorge of awe-inspiring cliffs.[2]

Nothing has yet occurred here to break the spell under which this spring and its close environment are held. The little house that stands in one corner, where cheese is made, is the same house, and the railing on one side to prevent you from falling into this allegedly bottomless pool, is the same old ugly railing. There is nothing else there to detract from the magic of the place. The water is cold but not clear. There is a milky

74

hue in its greenness. Is this because it comes from the Pheneos swamp on the other side of the high range of mountains through an underground passage? Pausanias says this:

> I heard that the water of the Phenean lake which drops into the potholes in the mountains comes up again here to form the springs of the Ladon. I am unable to say for certain whether that is the truth, but the Ladon has the finest water of any river in Greece, and besides this is famous in the world because of Daphne and her celebrated story.[3]

The water does indeed come from the marshy plain of what used to be the Pheneos lake which is why it tastes flat, as Frazer pointed out, not like the fresh water of a mountain spring. As for the story of Daphne, which Pausanias proceeds to relate, this is not the familiar one of Apollo's love for her and hopeless pursuit, but quite another unhappy love story, less known to the western world perhaps because it is not included in the *Metamorphoses* and so has failed to come to us through the renaissance.

> Oinomaos the lord of Pisa had a son called Leukippos who fell in love with Daphne, and knew he could never have her by straight wooing because she ran away from all men whatsoever, so he thought of a trick. Leukippos grew his hair long for the river Alpheius, so he plaited his long hair like a young virgin and put on women's clothes and went to Daphne and said he was Oinomaos's daughter and wanted to go hunting with her. She believed he was a virgin girl, a more brilliant huntress than the other girls, and of a much grander family, and besides he was extremely attentive to her, so that they became great friends. Those who celebrate Apollo as her lover add to all this that Apollo was jealous of Leukippos's success in love. So Daphne and the other young virgins wanted to swim in the Ladon, and stripped Leukippos against his will. When they saw that he was not a young girl, they stabbed him to death with their hunting knives and spears.[4]

According to Pausanias, Daphne was definitely a Ladon nymph and daughter of the river god.[5] For Parthenios, on the other hand, who relates the same story,[6] Daphne was the daughter not of Ladon but of Amyklas, king of Sparta. Parthenios' geography is much vaguer than Pausanias' and he concludes his account with Apollo's pursuit of Daphne and her transformation into a laurel tree, events that he regards as having taken place on the banks of a river in the Peloponnese, though he does not specify its name.

Closely connected with the Ladon is yet another unhappy love story, that of Pan and Syrinx, so charmingly told by Ovid through the words of Hermes. He makes him relate how the reed pipe was invented:

> 'In the chill mountains of Arcadia there lived a nymph, the most famous of all the wood nymphs of Nonacris. The other nymphs called her Syrinx. Many a time she had eluded the pursuit of satyrs and of other spirits who haunt the shady woodlands or the fertile

fields. She was a follower of the Ortygian goddess, imitating her in her pastimes, and in her virtue too. When she had her garments caught up out of the way, for hunting, as Diana wears hers, she could easily have been mistaken for Leto's daughter, save that her bow was of horn, Diana's of gold; even in spite of this, she used to be taken for the goddess.

'As she was returning from Mount Lycaeus Pan caught sight of her, Pan who wears on his head a wreath of sharp-leaved pine, and he spoke these words. ...' Mercury still had to tell what Pan said to the nymph and how she, scorning his prayers ran off through the pathless forest till she came to the still waters of sandy Ladon. When the river halted her flight, she prayed her sisters of the stream to transform her; and when Pan thought that he had at last hold of Syrinx, he found that instead of the nymph's body he held a handful of marsh reeds. As he stood, sighing, the wind blew through the reeds, and produced a thin plaintive sound. The god was enchanted by this new device and by the sweetness of the music. 'You and I shall always talk together so!' he cried; then he took reeds of unequal length, and fastened them together with wax. These preserved the girl's name.[7]

This is again a story of total dedication to virginity which all the nymphs that followed Artemis had to adopt, though not every one of them was insensitive to the stings of love. Kallisto succumbed and had to pay dearly for her weakness. Certainly florid Nonnos, who is regarded as decadent, kept disapproving of such obdurate virtue, at any rate before his conversion to Christianity:

For you know how Syrinx disregarded fiery Cythera and what price she paid for her too great pride and love for virginity; how she turned into a plant with reedy growth substituted for her own body, when she had fled from Pan's love and how she still sings Pan's desire! And how the daughter of Ladon, that celebrated river, hated the works of marriage and the nymph became a tree.[8]

The story of Syrinx and Pan is of Hellenistic vintage, for we have no reference to it before the Augustan age and none of the Greek writers of the Homeric and classical times mention it, though no doubt Ovid and Virgil had recourse to records that are now lost. There is something genuinely Arcadian about the story, with local roots which took time to flourish.

As a respectable river god, Ladon had of course distinguished offspring, but only daughters as far as I know. In addition to Daphne he had Merope, who married Asopos and was mother of very many celebrated children. He had also Thelpousa,[9] who gave her name to the city of Thelpousa situated close to the Ladon halfway down its course. Nearby there was a sanctuary of Demeter whom the Thelpousans, Pausanias tells us, called Fury.

When Demeter was wandering in search of her child, they say Poseidon followed her lusting to have intercourse with her, so she changed herself into a mare and grazed among the mares belonging to Onkios; but Poseidon saw how she tricked him and coupled with her in the form of a stallion. At that moment Demeter was very angry about what had happened though later on she got over her wrath and they say she fancied a wash in the Ladon, and this is how the goddess got her titles, the Fury because of her wrath, as the Arcadian expression for giving way to anger is to be furious, and Washing Demeter because she washed in the Ladon.[10]

About a mile or two below the confluence of the Aroanios with the Ladon, the latter receives the waters of another tributary, the Tragos, mentioned by Pausanias as issuing from a subterranean passage.[11] His geography, however, is somewhat confusing here. But there is indeed a plentiful spring on the road to Kalavrita from Tripolis a few miles before the confluence at the small village of Panaghitsa, which pours into the Tragos and is its main supply of water. The manner in which it emerges suggests that the water comes from afar underground. No mythological records concerning the Tragos have reached us, but *tragos* means 'he-goat', and indeed the banks of this river swarm with goats.

The middle course of the Ladon, which used to be impressive and was vividly described by Frazer in his commentary on Pausanias, has been much disturbed by the creation of an artificial lake and the installation of hydroelectric works, which have impaired the landscape. But below this injury the river resumes its natural course in unblemished surroundings until it joins the Alpheios at the border of Arcadia and Elis. Here another river flows in, the Erymanthos of no insignificant mythological importance. The confluence of the three streams is impressive and attractive. The waters of the Ladon sweep by, turbulent and muddy, flanked by willows and plane trees. The Erymanthos, much depleted by irrigation, is engulfed as soon as it touches the boisterous eddies of mighty Ladon which soon, however, calm down as they spread out into the smooth surface of the Alpheios (Plate 30).

CHAPTER

20

THE ERYMANTHOS
Haunt of Centaurs

HIGH ABOVE THE Erymanthos river, the archer Artemis, roamed the summits of Mount Erymanthos in pursuit of boars and swift deer. There she was joined in the chase by wood nymphs, so Homer tells us.[1] River and mountain share the same name, being closely related to each other both geographically and mythologically. It was in this region that Herakles hunted and caught alive the famous wild boar, his fourth labour. Pausanias tells us this:

> The Erymanthus has its springs on Mount Lampeia, which is said to be sacred to Pan. Lampeia would really be part of Mount Erymanthus. ... The river passes through Arcadia with Mount Pholoe on the right and Thelpousa on the left again, and flows into the Alpheius. It is said that Heracles at the orders of Eurystheus hunted a boar beside the Erymanthus, which surpassed all others in size and strength.[2]

The Erymanthos is a pleasant river which after receiving the contributary waters of two lesser streams at the present-day hamlet of Tripotamos, descends steeply into a defile, deep and wooded, under the dominating buttresses and offshoots of Mount Erymanthos known as the Pholoe range. It was once a haunt of the centaurs who had been expelled from Mount Pelion after the Lapiths conflict.

Down in the valley the river rushes along with plentiful water throughout the year, but by the time it joins the Alpheios it is nowadays much depleted by irrigation. From its banks the ground rises steeply to considerable heights, in a splendid setting with Mount Erymanthos looming in the northwest. The right bank escarpment rises more abruptly, however, and forms the Pholoe range which at the top flattens out into a plateau where today there is still a great forest of oak trees. In the woods overlooking the river lived the community of centaurs, and here, in pursuit of the boar, came Herakles who was received and entertained in his cave by Pholos, one of the chief centaurs. Herakles was offered roast meat to eat by Pholos, a good host, who personally preferred raw meat. Herakles then caught sight of a jar in a corner of the cave and so he clamoured for wine. Pholos hesitated, for the wine in the jar, he explained, belonged to the centaurs in common and he therefore feared to open it without their consent. But Herakles insisted. 'Come on Pholos, be of a good sport, let's have some wine.' Without further ado Herakles got hold of the jar, opened it and drank plentifully. He was evidently far gone when the other centaurs, smelling the wine from afar, came to the dwelling in a state of excitement. There followed a brawl in which Herakles behaved disgracefully, as he often did when he lost control of himself. Not only did he kill several of the centaurs, but after a bloody fight, in which poor terrified Pholos (who had unsuccessfully hidden in a corner of the cave) was mortally wounded, Herakles pursued the surviving centaurs who had escaped from the cave into the woods. They took refuge with the highly civilized centaur Chiron, who had been the teacher of most of the distinguished heroes in Greece. Obviously Herakles was drunk, for when he caught up with them he mistakenly shot Chiron, his old friend, with one of his poisonous arrows. Nessos managed to get away, but some years later he too came to an unhappy end at the hands of Herakles.[3]

Overlooking Tripotamos are situated the ruins of the ancient city of Psophis. Nearby, on the banks of the Erymanthos, stood a shrine which, according to Pausanias, contained a statue of the river god made of white stone, probably limestone.[4] In Pausanias' account there is an interesting observation about the stone of river statues, from which it is to be clearly deduced that river gods were not uncommonly represented in sculpture. Unfortunately most of these statues have not survived.

CHAPTER

21

THE ALPHEIOS

A River God Renowned for His Lust

THE ALPHEIOS, LARGEST of the Peloponnesian rivers, rises near Asea in the Megalopolitan territory of Arcadia. With various vicissitudes, including disappearing underground and emerging to the surface more than once, it flows through southern Arcadia and Elis, emptying itself into the Ionian Sea about ten miles west of Olympia. Of noble birth, such as every distinguished river god had to be, he received the attention of poets from the earliest ages as well as of mythographers, historians and geographers. As son of Okeanos and Tethys, Alpheios comes second, after the Nile, in Hesiod's catalogue of great rivers in the *Theogony*. But we find references to it already in Homer who mentions the river several times in the *Iliad*[1] and in the *Odyssey*,[2] sometimes in its capacity as river, and sometimes as a river god who received sacrifices such as, for instance, bulls. And again we find Alpheios mentioned in the Homeric Hymn to Hermes: 'The strong son of Zeus drove the wide-browed cattle of Phoebus Apollo to the river Alpheius. And they came unwearied to the high-roofed byres and the drinking-troughs that were before the noble meadows'[3] (Plate 32).

Just as certain notable events relating to Herakles took place in the waters and on the banks of the Evenos, others in connection with the Acheloös, so also some memorable deeds of the hero were closely related to the Alpheios. He cleansed the Augean stables by diverting into them the course of the river and thereby washing them out.[4] Moreover he founded the Olympic Games on the banks of the Alpheios, according to Diadoros Siculus.[5] Apart from Herakles it was said that Salmoneos, son of Aiolos, founded the city of Salmonia by the Alpheios in Elis.[6] And even Dionysus himself was believed by some to have been born on the banks of this river.[7]

Some river gods liked to lead a passive life, watching the events that took place on their banks, in which their daughters were often awkwardly involved, such as for instance Ladon, Evenos or Eurotas. But there were other river gods whose nature it was to be active in some form or other, such as Acheloös, Asopos of Phlios and indeed Alpheios. This deity was renowned for his amorous disposition. The most famous of his passionate loves was for the nymph Arethusa – a story which fascinated poets, mythographers, geographers, historians and travellers. Pausanias sums the story up in a few words:

There is a legend about Alpheius. They say there was a hunter called Alpheius, who fell in love with Arethusa, who was herself a huntress. Arethusa, unwilling to marry, crossed, they say, to the island opposite Syracuse called Ortygia and turned from a woman into a spring (Plate 34). This is the story of Alpheius reaching Ortygia. That Alpheius passes through the sea and mingles his waters with the spring of this place I cannot disbelieve, as I know that the god at Delphi confirms the story. For when he dispatched Archias, the Corinthian, to found Syracuse he uttered:

'An isle, Ortygia, lies on the misty sea
Over against Trinacria, where the mouth of Alpheius bubbles,
Mingling with the spring of broad Arethusa.'

For this reason, therefore, because the water of the Alpheius mingles with the Arethusan, I am convinced that the legend arose of the river's love affair.[8]

Ortygia was the ancient name of the island of Delos where Apollo was born. As his sister Artemis was also born there she was often called Ortygia and as she was greatly worshipped by the Syracusans, they called Ortygia the little island opposite the city which had a perennial spring sacred to her.

Hallowed spot, where Alpheius breathed again, Ortygia,
Scion of famous Syracuse,
Resting place of Artemis, sister of Delos.[9]

So exclaims Pindar with unshaken belief equal to that of Pausanias' in Alpheios' capacity to cross the sea under the surface. And Pliny was no less convinced that this was possible.[10]

But Strabo was highly sceptical. He says that the kind of evidence people adduce to prove that the Alpheios flows through the sea as far as the Syracusan island of Ortygia was based on a cup which, people said, had been thrown into the river near Olympia and which then came up in the fountain of Arethusa at Ortygia. Strabo then, in one of his debunking moods, proceeds to pull the myth to pieces:

If the Alpheius fell into a pit before joining the sea, there would be plausibility in the view that the stream extends underground from Olympia as far as Sicily, there preserving its potable water unmixed with the sea; but since the mouth of the river empties itself into the sea in full view, and since near the mouth, on the transit, there is no mouth visible that swallows up the stream of the river, the thing is absolutely impossible.[11]

Strabo, however, was demythologizing whereas we are moving in the world of myth. So let us see how Ovid tells the story of Alpheios and this huntress (another nymph dedicated to virginity as a follower of Artemis), through her own words which enable us to understand how a river god's lust could be aroused by the striptease of a nymph when she went swimming:

I used to be one of the nymphs who have their dwelling in Achaia, and no other was more eager in scouring the glades, or in setting the hunting nets. But although I never sought the fame of beauty, although I was brave, I had the name of beautiful. Nor did my beauty, all too often praised, give me any joy; and my dower of charming form, in which often maids rejoice, made me blush like a country girl, and I deemed it wrong to please. Wearied with the chase, I was returning, I remember, from the Stymphalian wood; the heat was great and my toil made it double. I came upon a stream flowing without eddy, and without sound, crystal-clear to the bottom, in whose depths you might count every pebble, waters which you scarcely think to be moving. Silvery willows and poplars fed by the water gave natural shade to the soft-sloping banks. I came to the water's edge and first dipped my feet; then I went up to the knees; not satisfied with this I removed my robes, and hanging the soft garments on a drooping willow, naked I plunged into the waters. And while I beat them, drawing them and gliding in a thousand turns, I thought I heard a kind of murmur deep in the pool. In terror I leapt on the nearer bank; the Alpheius called from his waters: 'Whither in haste, Arethusa? Whither in such haste?' Twice his hoarse voice called to me. As I was without my robes, I fled; for my robes were on the other bank. So much the more he pressed on and burned with love; naked I seemed readier for his taking. So did I flee and so did he hotly press after me, as doves on fluttering pinions flee the hawk, as the hawk pursues the frightened doves. Even past Orchomenos, past Psophis and Cyllene, past the woods of Maenalus, chill Erymanthus and Elis, I kept my flight; nor was he swifter of foot than I. But I, being ill-matched in strength, could not long keep up my speed, while he could sustain a long pursuit. Yet through level plains, over mountains covered with trees, over rocks also and cliffs, and where there was no way at all, I ran. The sun was at my back, I saw my pursuer's long shadow stretching out ahead of me – unless it was fear that I saw – but surely I heard the terrifying sound of feet, and his deep-panting breath fanned my hair. Then, forspent with toil of flight, I cried aloud: 'O help me, or I am caught, help thy armour-bearer, goddess of the hunt, to whom so often thou hast given thy bow to bear and they quiver, with all its arrows.' The goddess heard, and threw an impenetrable cloud about me. The river god circled around me, wrapped in the darkness, and at fault quested about the hollow mist. And twice he went round the place where the goddess had hidden me, unknowing, and twice he called, 'Arethusa! O Arethusa!' How did I feel then, poor wretch! Was I not the lamb, when it hears the wolves howling around the folds? Or the hare which, hiding in the bramble, sees the dogs' deadly muzzles and dares not make the slightest motion? But he went not far away, for he saw no traces of my feet further on; he watched the cloud and the place. Cold sweat poured down my beleagered limbs and the dark drops rained down from my whole body. Wherever I put my foot a pool trickled out, and from my hair fell the drops: and sooner than I can now tell the tale I was changed to a stream of water. But sure enough he recognized in the waters the maid he loved; and laying aside the form of a man which he had assumed, he changed back to his own watery shape to mingle with me. My Delian goddess cleft the earth, and I, plunging down into the dark depths, was borne hither to Ortygia, which I love because it bears my goddess's name, and this first received me to the upper air.[12]

If on this occasion it was a nymph, follower of Artemis, whom Alpheios sought to catch in his lustful embrace, it was the virgin goddess herself whom he tried to rape on another occasion. The story is told by Pausanias who, commenting on a statue of Alpheian Artemis which he saw in a temple at Letrini in Elis, says this:

This is how the goddess got her title: Alpheius fell in love with Artemis, and as he knew she would never marry him for prayers and persuasions he found the courage to try to violate the goddess: he came to a festival at Letrini which the goddess was holding with the nymphs who played with her. Artemis suspected what Alpheius was planning, and covered her face and all her nymphs' faces who were there with mud; when Alpheius arrived there was no way for him to tell Artemis from the others, and not being able to recognize her he went away with his purpose unfulfilled.[13]

The Alpheios flows through Elis, a broad river, not at all as clear as Ovid would have it, being full of silt, in a scenery of gentle hills with Mount Lykaion emerging above them far away to the south, amidst luxuriant vegetation consisting mainly of Aleppo pine, cypress and olive groves (Plate 32). It passes by Olympia which in the course of centuries became silted up and was virtually concealed before the site was excavated just over a hundred years ago. Not far from the ruins the Alpheios receives a small tributary, the Kladeos, which flows along the west side of the Altis holy precinct (Plate 35). Since nothing is known of its mythological past, it would be of little interest were it not that together with the Alpheios it is represented in human form on the east pediment of the Olympian temple of Zeus. The greater river god is seen represented in the left corner, the lesser one in the right corner (Plate 36). It appears that Kladeos was greatly revered. Pausanias describes their respective positions on the pediment as follows:

Cladeus is lying down at the very edge; Cladeus receives in general more honours in Elis than any other river except of course Alpheius. Left of Zeus are Pelops and Hippo-dameia and Pelops's driver and horses, and two men who must be Pelops's grooms. Just here where the pediment narrows towards its point, Alpheius is represented.[14]

These two reclining figures are undoubtedly of special interest in as much as they are amongst the extremely few river gods in Greek scuplture that have survived.

Some miles further west the Alpheios receives another modest stream which today is called Lestenitsa, but which most probably is the ancient Enipeus of Elis before it was known as the Barnichios in the days of Strabo who says this:

> Salmone is situated near the spring of that name from which flows the Enipeus river. The stream empties in the Alpheius and is now called the Barnichius. It is said that Tyro fell in love with Enipeus: 'She loved a river, the divine Enipeus'.[15]

Strabo's quotation is from Homer.[16] In relating his visit to Hades, Odysseos says:

> Then verily the first I saw was high-born Tyro, who said that she was the daughter of noble Salmoneus, and declared herself to be the wife of Getheus, son of Aeolus. She fell in love with the river, divine Enipeus, who is far the loveliest of rivers that send forth their streams upon earth, and she was wont to resort to the fair waters of Enipeus. But the Enfolder and Shaker of the earth took his form, and lay with her at the mouth of the river. And the dark wave stood about them like a mountain, vaulted over, and hid the god and the mortal woman. And he loosed her maiden girdle, and shed sleep upon her. But when the god had ended his work of love, he clasped her hand, and spoke and addressed her:
>
> 'Be glad, woman, in our love, and as the year goes on its course thou shalt bear glorious children, for not weak are the embraces of a god. These do then tender and rear. But now go to thy house, and hold thy peace, and tell no man; but know that I am Poseidon, the shaker of the earth.'[17]

Apollodoros tells the same story, though in less poetic terms,[18] and so does Diadoros Siculus.[19] But Lucian, in his flippant style, has left us an amusing dialogue between Enipeus and Poseidon which, I think, is worth quoting:

> *Enipeus*: A nice affair this, Poseidon, for the facts are these: You come along quite suddenly, surprising my girl right in front of me, and having taken my aspect rape her, and she, thinking that you are me, yields most willingly.
> *Poseidon*: Well, it all happened because you, Enipeus, were lazy and complacent; for the lovely girl kept talking to you every day, and you, watching her pining away with love, delighted in her anguish. She was roaming unhappily along your banks, swimming and bathing herself in your waters, longing to be possessed by you, and you did nothing about it.
> *Enipeus*: Was this good reason for your raping my sweetheart, for you Poseidon to appear in the form of me Enipeus, and in this manner to deceive this simple girl, Tyro?
> *Poseidon*: You are getting jealous too late, after having been so stuck-up, and besides Tyro hasn't suffered any ill since she thought she was being deflowered by you.
> *Enipeus*: Nonsense. This is not at all true since on leaving her you said you were Poseidon, which upset her a great deal, and I am all the more abused by your having enjoyed her in my stead under the purple ripples of water that covered you both.

Poseidon: All because of your neglect, Enipeus.[20]

The Alpheios has many tributaries and in describing the river's course Pausanias gives the names of the principal ones, all of which flow into it from its right side, or in other words from the north. He says:

> By the time you reach Olympia the Alpheius is a large and very pleasant river, being fed by several tributaries, including seven very important ones. The Helisson joins the Alpheius passing through Megalopolis; the Brentheates comes out of the territory of that city; past Gortyna, where there is a sanctuary of Asclepius, flows the Gortynius; from Melaeneae, between the territories of Megalopolis and Heraea, comes the Buphagus; from the land of the Clitorians the Ladon; from Mount Erymanthus a stream with the same name as the mountain. These come down into the Alpheius from Arcadia; the Cladeus from Elis to join it.[21]

Of these tributaries the Ladon and the Erymanthos are old friends. The Brentheates and the Buphagos are very minor streams, nowadays at any rate, virtually brooks, with no mythical past that we know of, and can therefore be discounted in our survey, but the Gortynios, usually known as the Lousios, is not only important as a tributary because of the volume of water it contributes to the Alpheios, but for other reasons as well. It is one of the most beautiful streams in Greece and its mythology is noteworthy.

> There is a river flowing through Gortys that people who live around its springs call the Lousios [the Wash], because it was used for washing Zeus at his birth, but people who live further from the springs call it the Gortynius after the name of the village. The Gortynius is the coldest water of any other river in the world.[22]

The Phigalians claimed that it was their river, the Neda, or its tributary the Lymax, in which Zeus was washed when he was born. No matter. Local rivalries.

The Gortynios, or Lousios, rises in the uplands of Dimitsana and flows for a couple of miles in a little green valley, a mere brook at this stage, and then, immediately below Dimitsana, pours over a rim into a deep limestone gorge. Here, fed on its precipitous descent by innumerable springs, it assumes the character of an abundant stream impetuously pouring from rock to rock and from pool to pool in a scenery of majestic grandeur. The sheer cliffs on either side seem to rise higher and higher above the headlong drop. Monasteries cling to them, and the now-deserted caves of hermits, carved into the rock, gape open in dismay. Here and there the silhouette of a cypress tree rears itself against the russet and ochre background from wherever soil has contrived to collect. In the deep cleft where the stream roars by icy cold, as Pausanias says, and crystal clear, there are waterfalls and deep pools (Plate 27), overhung with branches of plane trees, ilexes, laurel, willows, hornbeams and elms, the rocks festooned with creepers and ferns. The white boulders tumble over each other, many covered with moss, and the water tears along between them, foaming, frothing and roaring

wildly, intermittently subsiding for a rest in large pools of the deepest blue (Plate 28).
Here the boulders, now peacefully still, smile in the sun, inviting you to stretch on their
smooth surfaces or nestle in the curves of their bodies and there caress the textures of
their limbs moulded by the wash of the water. But the foaming chase is resumed in
pursuit of some virgin huntress unwilling to yield. The banks arch over at one point
of the course, the rock from either side is welded into a vault below which the numinous
powers of the stream convene in the shadows of the river god's abode. The sunlight
is only reflected from the white surface of a boulder to light up, like a torch, the august
presence. Here indeed the infant Zeus may have been washed.

Something strange happens a few miles further south, past the ruins of ancient
Gortys, where the gorge opens out into a green valley of prickly kermes, forsaking
olive trees. The Lousios, shaded by its plane trees and as clear as ever, sweeps along
the bottom of the valley under the brow of Karitena and its towering castle, until it
reaches the Alpheios. Here, at the confluence, their waters meet, but without mingling
at first, as though enmity kept them apart. From a virtually inaccessible crag overlooking
their encounter I watched the conflict. The dark waters of the Alpheios strove to
penetrate, with many coils and whirls, the clear blue water of the Lousios, which
bravely pushed them away in a struggle to preserve its identity. But in the end having
to succumb, it was engulfed.

Further up its course the Alpheios receives another few tributaries, which flow with
very little water however; in the summer they are often dry. But of these the Helisson,
which rises in the Mainalon heights, celebrated haunt of Pan, and passes by Megalopolis,
deserves some attention perhaps, not only because Pausanias mentions it several times
but also on account of its connection with the myth of Kallisto. Her grave, according
to Pausanias a high mound with a sanctuary of Artemis Kallisto on top, was situated
not far from the upper reaches of the Helisson in the folds of Mount Mainalon.[23] It
is therefore not unreasonable to assume that Kallisto was swimming here when,
according to Hesiod,[24] Hera discovered her pregnant in consequence of having been
made love to by Zeus. Enraged, the goddess changed her into a bear. But evidently
before she was turned into a constellation – the Great Bear – she gave birth to a son,
Arkas, from whom the Arcadians received their name. *Arktos* means 'bear' in ancient
Greek; in modern Greek the word is *arkouda*.

When I visited the Helisson in this region I was most disappointed to find it as dry
as the Inachos, possibly as a result of present-day irrigation methods.

About fifteen miles to the south of this area are situated the springs of the Alpheios,
near the ancient site of Asea, about which there has been much speculation because
of the ancient belief that the source of the Alpheios and that of the Eurotas were close
to each other. Pausanias says this:

Half a mile from Asea the head-spring of the Alpheius lies a little away from the road,

32 The Alpheios, largest of the Peloponnesian rivers, is frequently described by Homer as both river and river god. It was the waters of the Alpheios which Herakles diverted, presumably with the acquiescence of the river god, to make them flow through and thus cleanse the Augean stables.

33 Alpheios the river god was renowned for his lust. His pursuit of the nymph Arethusa – unsuccessful as it turned out – spawned a variety of myths, with Greek and later Roman writers often in dispute with each other about the authenticity of one or other version.

34 Arethusa, the nymph pursued by the river god Alpheios, in one version of the myth escapes to Sicily – hence her depiction here on a coin of Syracuse – where she was transformed into a spring. The amorous Alpheios then streamed through the sea, forced his path to the shores of Sicily and mingled his waters with those of the Arethusa spring there.

35 The Kladeos, a small tributary of the Alpheios, was revered by the inhabitants of Olympia.

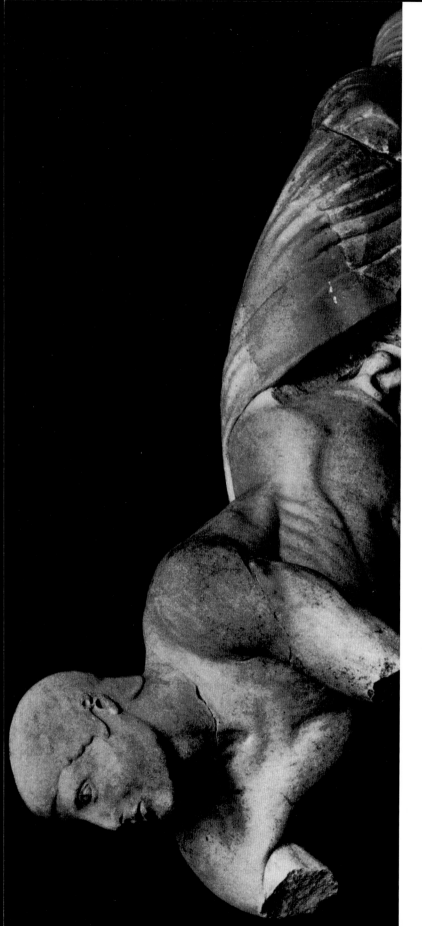

36 The river god Kladeos's mythological past is now not known to us, but his human representation stretching out on the east pediment of the Temple of *Zeus* at Olympia suggests that he must have been much favoured in the pantheon of deities.

37 The Eurotas, seen here in its upper reaches, is a placid river which nevertheless was prominent in mythology, literature and art. The river god Eurotas, true to the nature of the river's flow, preferred the passive role of observer rather than participant in the frequent sexual frolicking on the river's banks.

38 Zeus transformed himself into a swan to seduce Leda, mother of Helen, as she swam in the Eurotas. This fifth-century BC Greek relief was a precursor to the many representations of Leda's seduction by Zeus as a swan which have been made through the ages by artists including Leonardo da Vinci and Michelangelo. (© British Museum)

39 The Neda, flowing through the Peloponnese into the Ionian Sea, originated as a nymph who, according to the Arcadia tradition, assisted the goddess Rhea to give birth to Zeus in Arcadia (rather than in Crete). In the local traditions of Arcadia at least the Neda's role in helping to bring the god of gods into the world inspired a special reverence for the river.

40 The upper waterfall on the Lymax river, a tributary of the Neda, forms a natural sanctuary which in another version of the myth was the site of Zeus' birth – again leading to a degree of reverence.

and the source of the Eurotas is right at the road side. ... The stream of the Eurotas mingles with the Alpheius and they run together for two and a half miles, then they drop into a chasm, and the Eurotas comes up again in the country of Laconia and the Alpheius at Pegai, the Springs, in the Megalopolitan territory.[25]

With a more matter-of-fact approach and a grain of scepticism, Strabo makes the following remark in writing about underground streams:

> The water near Asea is first forced below the surface and then, much later, emerges as both the Eurotas and the Alpheius; hence the belief in a certain fabulous utterance, that if two wreaths be dedicated separately to each of the two rivers and thrown into the common stream, each will reappear, in accordance with the dedication, in the appropriate river.[26]

The assumption that the waters of two rivers could happily travel together without mixing must have stemmed from the belief in the divinity of rivers. A river god could not possibly lose his identity no matter how closely in contact he might come with another river god. The numerous potholes into which the waters of that region of Arcadia sink, re-emerging elsewhere as streams from apparent springs, give rise to any amount of fabulous as well as topographical speculation. Concerning the Alpheios, Pausanias makes the following relevant remark: 'It is known that the Alpheius differs from other rivers in exhibiting this natural peculiarity: it often disappears to reappear again.'[27] He also says, among other things, that the waters of the Alpheios sink in the Tegean plain and come up again at Asea. Indeed, a few miles west of Tegea, and about the same distance south of Tripolis, is Lake Takka, sometimes a mere marsh, but usually an attractive sheet of water bordered by great poplars and willows. On its western edge, right under a cliff, is a *katavothra*, or chasm, into which the water of the lake sinks underground. I think there can be little doubt that this is the main source of the so-called springs of the Alpheios near Asea and of the Eurotas at Lougaras under Mount Chelmos on the Lakonian border.

22

THE EUROTAS
Ancestor of Helen

The famous Lakonian river, 'the fair-flowing', is mentioned by neither Homer nor Hesiod; only later poets refer to it. Nevertheless the pedigree of the river god Eurotas was ancient.

> The Laconians themselves say that Lelex who was a child of the earth was the first king of this country, and that the Leleges whom he governed were named after him. Lelex had a son called Miles and a younger son Polycaon. ... When Miles died his son Eurotas inherited the sovereignty.[1]

Pausanias goes on to say that Eurotas had no male children and so he left the kingdom to Lakedaimon who had married his daughter Sparta. The city he founded was called after her. Tyndareos, king of Sparta, was a descendant of Lakedaimon, and father of Helen by his wife Leda, unless Zeus was her father, who had seduced Leda and made love to her as a swan. So, at any rate officially, Eurotas was Helen's ancestor. Klytaimnestra, however, was definitely the daughter of Tyndareos and Leda. But as for their brothers, the Dioskouroi, there was some doubt. Apollodoros says that Leda, having had sexual intercourse with Zeus and Tyndareos in succession on the same night, bore Pollux and Helen to Zeus, and Kastor and Klytaimnestra to Tyndareos.[2]

Stranded in Egypt, Helen bemoans her family's fate in Euripides' eponymous drama as follows:

> While for anguish at my deed of shame, hath Leda sought her death by hanging; and on the deep, to weary wandering doomed, my lord has met his end; Castor and his brother, twin glory of their native land, are vanished from man's sight, leaving the

plains that shook to their galloping steeds and the course beside the reed-fringed Eurotas, where those youthful athletes strove.[3]

The Eurotas was indeed celebrated for its banks where young athletes convened to swim in the river, to wrestle and gallop along on horseback, and where superior horses were bred. One went to fetch 'horses from the Eurotas abounding in mint'.[4] The youths of Sparta would meet there and emerge from their contests wreathed in garlands.[5] Not only youths, however, but also the young girls of Sparta would meet on the banks of the Eurotas to swim in its waters and, not unlike the men, engage in similar sport. So at the wedding of Helen her epithalamy was sung by her attendant maidens who:

> Ran with her the race,
> Anointed lasses like the lads,
> Eurotas' pools beside.[6]

A few miles south of Sparta is the site of Amyklai, an ancient sanctuary on top of a little hill close to the Eurotas. Here, Pausanias tells us,[7] was the tomb of the unfortunate son of King Lakedaimon, Hyakynthos, whose story was popularized by Ovid in his *Metamorphoses*. Apollodoros says that Thamyris, who was the first man to become enamoured of males, conceived a passion for the beautiful young Hyakynthos.[8] But it was a god who then fell in love with him and unwittingly caused his death. Apollo and the young man were playfully competing with each other on the banks of the Eurotas in hurling the discus, their bodies 'gleaming with olive oil', when Hyakynthos was accidentally struck and killed by the god's discus. Apollo burst into lamentation and, behold:

> The blood, which had poured out on the ground and stained the grass, ceased to be blood and in its place there sprang a flower brighter than Tyrian dye. It took the form of the lily, save that one was of purple hue, while the other was silvery white.[9]

But it was not only athletic contests and races that the Eurotas experienced on its banks and in its waters, for it also drew gods, men, women and nymphs to engage in another pleasant activity, hardly a mere sport, that of lovemaking, which indeed beautiful rivers were in the habit of encouraging. So, for instance, Poseidon was tempted to choose a ford of the Eurotas to accost and lie with the nymph Pitane,[10] who as a result gave birth to Evadne. She, in her turn, was made pregnant by Apollo on the banks of the Alpheios. But one of the most famous love encounters of that kind took place by the river Eurotas (Plate 37). It occurred in its very waters, between a god and a mortal woman, not a nymph. Indeed it was Helen's own mother, Tyndareos' wife, who was seduced by Zeus while bathing in the Eurotas. He came to her in the form of a swan. We find this remarkable event, which became such an alluring subject for artists through the centuries, first mentioned by Euripides in his *Helen*; there, at the outset of the drama, the exiled queen of Sparta says by way of introducing herself, 'A legend tells how Zeus winged his way to my mother Leda's breast, in the semblance of a bird, even a swan.'[11]

The swan could appear in a fifth-century BC relief (Plate 38) as a rapacious bird of great size grasping a submissive Leda by the nape of her neck with its beak, holding her down and gripping her thighs with its webbed feet; or, in a famous picture attributed to Leonardo da Vinci, as a rather coy and comic-looking fowl standing up at a discrete distance from Leda, with its laid eggs on the ground which are breaking open and giving birth to Pollux and Helen; or as a lascivious swan between the legs of a reclining and delighted-looking young lady in the nude to whose lips it reaches up with its beak, an interpretation of the event that can be seen in the copies of a painting by Michelangelo now lost; or, for instance, it comes to life again as a very suggestive feathered creature in the imagination of a prominent poet of more recent times:

> A sudden blow: the great wings beating still
> Above the staggering girl, her thighs caressed
> By the dark webs, her nape caught in his bill,
> He holds her helpless breast upon his breast.
>
> How can those terrified vague fingers push
> The feathered glory from her loosening thighs?
> And how can body, laid in that white rush,
> But feel the strange heart beating where it lies?[12]

No doubt Yeats must have been inspired by the British Museum relief, of which there is a very similar version in the National Museum of Athens.

So the fame of Eurotas has come down to us from time immemorial as a river which played an eminent part in mythology, literature and art, but as a passive river god who watched the events that took place on his banks or in his stream, rather than an active, participant deity. As for the whole landscape of Sparta, in which the Eurotas still plays its part, Edward Dodwell, who visited the region at the beginning of the nineteenth century, described it as follows:

> The plain, as viewed from Sparta, assumes an oblong appearance, glowing with every tint that nature so profusely blends when she means most to charm the eye and delight the mind, while its natural attractions are increased by assiduous cultivation. The level surface of the plain is interrupted by small hills, or broken into occasional intervals of picturesque ruggedness. This scenery is enlivened by the lucid current of the Eurotas gliding close to the ruins, and gently meandering towards the south, where it loses itself at the distance of several miles amongst the undulating hills of Maina, which intercept the view of the Laconian gulf, the Taenarian promontory and the port of Gythion.[13]

Chateaubriand, who was there in 1806, has left us an even more glowing description of the Eurotas, such as he found it in his day:

I climbed down the acropolis and walked for about a quarter of an hour to reach the Eurotas. It was approximately such as I had seen it two miles further up its course without realizing what river it was. At Sparta it may have the width of the Marne before Charenton. The river bed, practically dry in summer, is shingly, full of reeds and oleander. Over it flow some streaks of cool and limpid clear water. It seemed excellent to me and I drank of it abundantly, as I was dying of thirst. The Eurotas merits the epithet 'kallidonax', or beautiful reeds, which Euripides has given it, but I don't know whether it should retain that of oloriferus since I didn't see any swans in its waters. I followed its course in the hope of finding these birds which, according to Plato, are granted the sight of Mount Olympus before they die, which is why their last song is so melodious. My search was abortive. Evidently, unlike Horace, I am not favoured by the Tyndarids who didn't allow me to penetrate the secret of their cradle. Celebrated rivers have the same destiny as celebrated nations. First unknown, then famous all over the world, they eventually slip back into their former obscurity.[14]

François Pouqueville, who visited Lakonia about the same time, expressed his feelings on coming in sight of the Eurotas with even greater emotion:

A little river called by turns the Chelesina and the Pitani, and which runs into the Eurotas, is twice crossed at short distance from its source. Scarcely do we quit these abodes, where the silence is only interrupted by the warbling of innumerable feathered songsters, when a new spectacle opens upon us. We approach the Royal River, we follow the course of its banks, we see the ancient sight of Sparta about a league before us, with the mountains of Mistra and the castle that crowns it; the town is not, however, to be seen. Some villages with some long tracts of vines are the principal objects which present themselves to the attention of the traveller in a corner of the world once so celebrated, but in these days scarcely known. He salutes the cherished woods of Diana, he hails with rapture the laurels that border the Eurotas, he still finds the reeds which served the Spartans for beds, for arrows, for pens. Slowly he proceeds anxious to examine in detail the minutest objects; he approaches the river, its waters still roll unimpeded fowards, they pursue the same course that they had pursued for so many ages; we still see them, we still contemplate them – but where are the warlike race who so long inhabited these banks? Of them we know that they once did exist.

Later in his account Pouqueville finds occasion to describe the little island called 'the platanist', because of its plane trees:

The platanist mentioned above must not be slightly passed over; some further homage must be paid to this delightful little island. It is still planted in the centre with plane trees; on its borders are weeping willows and citruses hanging over and reflected in the water, while tufts of rose trees, of laurels, of silk trees scattered about charm the eye and perfume the air. ... It was here in this island, along the banks of the river by which it is bathed, that according to Theocritus the flowers were gathered to form the garland with which Helen was crowned on the day of her marriage.[15]

In those days modern Sparta had not yet been built. What would Dodwell,

91

Chateaubriand or Pouqueville say of the Eurotas at Sparta today? The sprawling new concrete buildings, the power cables, pylons, telephone wires and poles, the tarmac roads, cars, lorries, bulldozers and tractors, as well as the tourist invasion and ubiquitous plastic litter, have all combined to change the visual character not only of the region, populous and thrifty as it is, but also of the river itself. A trickle of water still flows but it is of a yellowish hue far from lucid, let alone drinkable, and the banks of the stream scarcely retain a breath of that idyllic atmosphere they once emanated with such profusion. The background scenery is as magnificent as ever, one of the most beautiful landscapes in the world. But if we wish to find the Eurotas where it is still possible to conjure up from the past a picture of Leda being approached by an amorous swan, as she emerges naked from the clear water of the stream on its bank shaded by willows and poplars, we should look for it a long way away upstream, near the source (Plate 37) or at the very spring itself under Lakonian Mount Chelmos.

23

THE PAMISOS

A River God of Some Importance

PEER OVER THE mountains. What is there on the other side of the Taygetos range? What about the Pamisos in Messenia, which Strabo says is the largest river in the Peloponnese? He adds, however, that it is no more than a hundred stadia in length, or about fifteen miles, from its source, which doesn't seem very long. It flows, he says, with abundance of water through the Messenian plain.[1] Nowadays the river is much longer because instead of starting from the lake that probably still existed in Strabo's times immediately northeast of Mount Ithome, it rises further north in the mountains bordering with Arcadia. But to call it a large river, let alone the largest in the Peloponnese, is an absurd exaggeration. Such as it displays itself today the Pamisos is a niggardly stream, though its present aspect may be very different from what it used to be like when it flowed 'with abundance of water'. Pausanias qualifies further the nature of the river such as it then was, stressing the clarity of its waters.

> The Pamisus is a pure stream flowing through cultivated lands, and is navigable some ten stades from the sea. Sea fish run up it, especially in spring, as they do up the Rhine and Maeander. The chief run of fish is up the Acheloüs, which discharges opposite the Echinades islands. But the fish that enter the Pamisus are of a quite different kind, as the water is pure and not muddy like the rivers which I have mentioned.[2]

So as well as being navigable the Pamisos flowed beautifully clear, as Pausanias tells us, through land already in his days intensely cultivated, for the Messenian plain has always been extremely fertile. But evidently modern methods of farming and irrigation have depleted the river and rendered its waters both shallow and murky, with not much beauty left on its banks. Its mythological past, concerning which hardly any records have survived, remains obscure. The Pamisos, in fact, would hardly be worth any consideration at all were it not for a remark Pausanias makes in passing, namely that the river was a god of some importance for whom an institution was founded by the king of Messenia for the purpose of offering the deity yearly sacrifices.[3]

CHAPTER

24

THE NEDA AND THE LYMAX

Where Zeus Was Born?

And holden in distress the lady Rhea said: 'Dear Earth, give birth thou also! Thy birth pangs are light.' So spake the goddess, and lifting her great arm aloft she smote the mountain with her staff; and it was greatly rent in twain for her and poured forth a mighty flood. Therein, O Lord, she cleansed thy body; and swaddled thee, and gave thee to Neda to carry within the Cretan covert, that thou mightest be reared secretly. Neda, eldest of the nymphs who were about her bed, earliest birth after Styx and Philyra. And no idle favour did the goddess repay her, but named that stream Neda.[1]

FROM THIS SPRING, which pregnant Rhea brought into existence by striking the earth on the slopes of Mount Lykeion before giving birth to Zeus, according to the Arcadian tradition, the river Neda emerges and flows westward through a deep and beautiful valley into the Ionian Sea. The whole territory of Mount Lykaion, that wonderful scenery of ridges wild and rugged, of oaks and plane trees, of glens and glades where Lykaion reigned and his iniquitous sons committed the crime of offering Zeus, their guest, the roasted flesh of a child,[2] is a region fraught with springs of myth. As you roam these mountains and strike the ground with your staff like Rhea, they seem to well up wherever you go on your wandering way down to the Neda. High up to the north, on the crest of Mount Kotilion overlooking the valley, is the temple of

95

Bassai, and down in the valley near the river itself are the remains of Phigaleia, the city that had the temple erected. The Neda, which flows with plentiful water throughout the year amongst boulders and through narrow rocky clefts, is one of the most delightful and as yet unspoilt streams of Greece. This is because, for most of its course, it can only be reached on foot down very rough and steep paths (Plate 39). It is therefore still untouched by litter, unblemished by discarded plastic bags, the scourge of modern Greece.

The river runs down to the sea, forming the boundary between northwestern Messenia, southwestern Arcadia and southern Elis, thus giving rise to rival claims in the world of mythology. Strabo gives us a geographical description of the river's course,[3] which formed somewhat complex borders between territories and peoples, while Pausanias makes the following remark on the subject of mythological rivalries:

> It is a hopeless task, however zealously undertaken, to enumerate all the people who claim that Zeus was born and brought up among them. The Messenians have their share in the story; for they say that the god was brought up among them and that his nurses were Ithome and Neda, the river having received its name from the latter, while the former, Ithome, gave her name to the mountain.[4]

On the other hand the Arcadians, according to Pausanias,[5] claimed that Zeus was not reared in Crete but on Mount Lykaion. They said, moreover, that the nymphs who looked after him were Theisoa, Neda and Hago, and that the river received its name from Neda.

We may assume that this nymph became then identified with the river, as in the case of King Inachos and the river called after him, which would mean that the Neda is one of the very few streams that were female deities. This is not certain, however, since we find on some Phigalian coins the river Neda represented as a male figure.[6] In any case the Phigalians honoured their river deity, to whom they made offerings.

On the subject of the exact locality of Zeus's birth Pausanias gives us some further information of interest:

> A stream called the Lymax flowing beside Phigalia empties itself into the Neda, and the river, they say, got its name from the cleansing of Rhea. For when she gave birth to Zeus the nymphs who cleansed her up after her travail threw the refuse into the river. Now the ancients called refuse *lymata*, as proved by Homer when he says that the Greeks were cleansed after the plague had come to an end, and threw the *lymata* in the sea[7]. The source of the Neda is on Mount Kerausion, which is part of Mount Lycaeon. At the point where the Neda comes closest to the city of Phigalia, the boys cut off their hair as an offering to the river.

A little further on, Pausanias adds a few fascinating details:

> Some twelve stades above Phigalia are hot baths and not far from these the Lymax falls

into the Neda. Where the streams meet is the sanctuary of Eurynome holy from ancient times, hard to get at because of the roughness of the ground. Around it are many cypress trees growing close together. Eurynome is believed by the people of Phigalia to be the surname of Artemis, but students of ancient records say Eurynome is a daughter of Oceanus, whom Homer mentions in the Iliad, saying that along with Thetis she received Hephaestus. On the same day in each year they open the sanctuary of Eury-nome, but at any other time it is a transgression for them to open it. On that day though, they offer sacrifices privately and publicly. I didn't arrive at the time of the festival and I did not see the statue of Eurynome; but the Phigalians told me that golden chains bind the wooden image, which represents a woman down to the buttocks, and below that like a fish. As the daughter of Oceanus, living with Thetis in the depths of the sea, the fish may be regarded as a kind of emblem of her. But there could be no probable connection between such a shape and Artemis.[8]

Pausanias' conclusion is correct, but the interesting thing about this Eurynome of Phigaleia is that she was represented as a mermaid, something exceptional since a mermaid – a sea creature half female human and half fish – is a Northern conception, on the whole alien to the Mediterranean. We don't find them in Greek mythology, at any rate playing a significant part. The Nereids and Naiads had bodies entirely human and the Sirens were partly bird. This Eurynome, however, before the pundits and priests started calling her such and associating her with the Homeric and Hesiodic Eurynome, was most probably a local river nymph with a body like a mermaid's. The fish part may have represented a Neda trout, a most appropriate emblem for that locality.

Pausanias says there were hot baths about twelve stades, or approximately one and a half miles, 'above' Phigaleia, and that not far from them the Lymax falls into the Neda. There are no traces today of such baths anywhere within that distance or beyond, and I don't think he could have meant twelve stades upstream, where there is nothing very much in the way of tributaries, rivers or even little streams. I think he meant by above 'higher up', probably somewhere near the present-day village of Stomion, which is situated to the west of Phigaleia at about that very distance, for nearby a stream does fall steeply into the Neda at a very rugged and rocky (trachytetos) spot, 'hard to get at'. Pausanias says the Lymax actually 'falls' (kateisin) into the Neda and here indeed that stream pours into it forming a waterfall. It must therefore be the Lymax. The whole site has an awe-inspiring, numinous character which answers most vividly Pausanias' description. The Neda, at this stage of its course, passes through a deep, narrow and rocky cleft only a few metres wide and most difficult to descend into, the sides being virtually sheer. At a short distance beyond the Lymax waterfall the Neda disappears into a tunnel of rock about three hundred feet or more in length, which is locally known as the Stomion or Orifice. On the right bank above it, the sanctuary of Eurynome may well have stood, where there is now an abandoned chapel inhabited by hundreds of bats, immediately beyond which signs of an ancient religious cult can be seen in the rock of the cliff.

The Lymax has more than one waterfall. Above the brim, over which it pours down into the Neda, a pool is formed under another smaller waterfall. Above this, if you scramble steeply up the side through prickly herbs and over rocks strewn with dry, slippery kermes leaves, clutching at overhanging branches of trees or protruding roots to pull yourself up the perpendicular parts of your ascent, suddenly there opens out before you, as you reach more level ground, a wondrous sight. A deep blue-green pool lays itself open in a parting of the plane trees, ilexes and evergreen maples which enclose it but for the far end. There, a dazzling white waterfall manifests itself, about thirty feet high, shimmering like a sheet of silk in the sun, which with reflected light illumines the surface of water in the circular enclosure of trees and rocks mottled with moss (Plate 40). This is indeed a sanctuary, totally sequestered, which nature has built, Rhea's sanctuary, even if no record has come down to us from ancient times. For here, more than anywhere else, you can capture the vision of Rhea giving birth to Zeus, helped by her nymphs who, after her travail, wash her and throw the placenta into the Lymax. All you can do is to sit in awe on a rock and gaze in silence. In silence? Yes in silence but for a gentle murmur. Isn't it, however, in the nature of waterfalls to resound with noise? Not here, in Rhea's sanctuary. You may wonder why, though at first, in the spellbinding atmosphere of mystery in which you find yourself, you are almost ready to accept it as a fairylike wonder wrought by the goddess. But then, after a survey, you discover the cause, a natural one. The water glides down, at the speed of falling water, however, as far as the eye can tell, over a surface of white lime deposit almost, but not entirely, perpendicular, which softens the impact of the fall.

The numinous atmosphere of the place is not only due to natural beauty but also, and no less, to the myth of Rhea giving birth here to Zeus, which clings to the site like moss to the rock, fills the air you breathe and informs the water, the trees, the stones, the very earth.

In bringing to a close this survey of the river gods of Greece I allow myself to quote a paragraph on the numinous in nature from a short story I wrote some years ago:

The numinous is the life of wonder that rises in waves from the mystery of a place blessed by the gods and loved by man. It rises airborne to the snow-clad peaks of the gods and sinks deep into the heart of man. It needs the earth to push its roots into and shoot up from, but it needs no less both God and man to grow, to live, to be what it is and make itself felt.[9]

MYTHOLOGICAL RIVERS AND OTHER STREAMS OF INTEREST

Acheloös river,	2, 8, 9–14, 19, 33, 80, 81, 93; source of, 13
Acheron river,	15–26, 30
Aoös river,	27, 28, 29
Arachthos river,	19, 27, 29, 30
Aroanios river,	72–3
Asopos river, Boeotian,	31, 46, 50–1
Asopos river, of Phleius,	67–8, 81
Axios river,	9, 31, 40, 41, 42
Bolinaios torrent,	58, 66
Boura torrent,	58, 66
Dyras river,	45, 46
Echeidoros river,	41
Enipeus stream, of Elis,	84, 85
Enipeus river,	34, 39
Erasinos river,	61–2, 68
Erymanthos river,	77, 78–9, 85
Eurotas river,	62, 81, 87, 88–92
Evenos river,	2, 8, 21–6, 80, 81

Haliakmon river, 40
Hyllikos river, 3, 57, 63–4
Ilissos river, 31, 52–6
Inachos river, 3, 13, 52, 57, 59–60, 86
Kephisos river, of Attica, 2, 31, 52–6
Kephisos river, of Boeotia, 47–9
Kladeos, stream, 54, 83
Kokytos river, 17, 18, 20
Krathis river, 58, 66, 70
Krathis stream, 58, 59
Ladon river, 2, 67, 74–7, 81, 85
Louros river, 29
Lousios river, 29, 35, 85, 86
Lymax river, 3, 29, 85, 95–8
Neda river, 2, 29, 85, 95–8
Nestos river, 33, 40, 43
Pamisos river, 34, 93–4
Peneios river, 2, 31, 33–9, 40, 60
Selemnos stream, 58, 65
Selinos stream, 58, 66
Spercheios river, 2, 31, 44–6
Strymon river, 31, 40, 41, 42, 43
Styx river, 16, 20, 35, 66, 69–71, 95
Thyamis river, 28, 62
Titaressos river, 35, 40
Tragos river, 77
Voidomati river, 27, 28

NOTES

Except where otherwise stated, all translations are my own. All references to Loeb are to the Loeb Classical Library.

Introduction

1. Homer *Iliad*, XX.4–9.
2. Homer *Iliad*, XI.27; XXI.135; XXIII.141, 147; Aeschylus *Choeph* 6; Pausanias I.37.2; VIII.41.3.
3. Pausanias V.10.6; VIII.24.12.
4. Virgil *Georgics* IV.317f.
5. Unfortunately irrigation schemes, the construction of dams and artificial lakes, the deviation of streams for agricultural purposes and other forms of development are seriously affecting the ecology and character of the rivers in Greece. The rivers and their landscape are constantly being threatened and in several cases have suffered regrettable change.

1. The Acheloös: Greece's Great River, Rich in Myths

1. Hesiod *Theogony* 340.
2. Homer *Iliad* III.191ff.
3. Apollodoros I.III.4.
4. Homer *Iliad*, XXIV.616 (Loeb).
5. Apollodoros, III.7.5 (Loeb).
6. Pausanias X.8.5.
7. Euripides *Bacchae* 519.
8. Pindar frag. 249b (Loeb).
9. Sophocles *Trachiniae* 7–8 (trans. R.C. Jebb, Random House, New York).
10. Sophocles *Trachiniae* 508ff (trans. R.C. Jebb, Random House, New York).
11. Ovid *Metamorphoses* IX.62ff. (trans. M.M. Innes, Penguin 1955).
12. There is another version of the myth concerning the origin of the cornucopia, according to which it was one of the horns of Amaltheia, the goat nurse of Zeus; Apollodoros II.7.4–5. A goat's horn, however, is much too small to be a symbol of plenty or, in other words, a horn big enough to contain flowers and fruit in abundance. Diadoros Siculus IV.34.4, confuses the two versions, but stresses the

symbolism of fertility derived from the waters of a river and irrigation. The Hellenized image of the Nile in marble, which the Romans took away from Alexandria, reclines upon a cornucopia. Thereafter the river god Tiber would be represented on the fountains of Rome grasping a cornucopia. In the Renaissance the cornucopia, as a symbol of fertility where water abounds, comes back into sculpture. On the fountain of Ammanati in Florence the Gianbologna nymphs hold firmly the cornucopia.

13. Herodotus X.10 (trans. G. Rawlinson, Everyman/Dent, London 1940).
14. Thucydides II.102 (trans. R. Crawley, Everyman/Dent, London 1940).
15. Strabo X.2.19 (Loeb).
16. Thucydides II.102.
17. Strabo VI.2.4.
18. Not to be confused with the Inachos of Argolis.
19. Strabo VII.7.7.
20. Apollodoros III.7.5–7.

2. The Acheron: River of the Underworld

1. Apollodoros I.5.3.
2. Homer *Odyssey* XI.14.
3. Homer *Odyssey* X.509.
4. Herodotus V.92.7 (trans. G. Rawlinson, Everyman/Dent, London 1940).
5. Euripides *Alcestis* 435ff. (trans. R. Aldington, Random House 1938).
6. Pausanias XIV-2 (Loeb).
7. Homer *Iliad* XIII.389 and XVI.482.
8. Apollodoros II.7.6 (Loeb).
9. Sophocles *Antigone* 8LL.
10. Strabo VII.7.5–6.
11. Homer *Odyssey* I.256.
12. Pausanias I.27.4–5.
13. Plato *Phaedon* 112ff. (trans. Henry Cary, Everyman 1947).
14. Virgil *Aeneid* VI.
15. Thucydides I.46 (trans. R. Crawley, Everyman/Dent, London 1940).
16. Henry Holland *Travels in the Ionian Islands*, London 1815.
17. Aristophanes *The Frogs* 474.
18. The charcoal-burners and their mules have vanished in recent years as a result of modern facilities, gas and motorized transport.

3. The Kokytus: The Other River of the Underworld

1. Homer *Odyssey* X.514 (Loeb).
2. Plato *Phaedo* 112ff.
3. Pausanias 1.7.4–5.

4. The Evenos: Where Nessos Was Killed

1. Apollodoros I.7.8–9; Hyginus *Fab*.242; Scholiast and Eustathios on *Iliad* IX.557.
2. Apollodoros I.8.1.
3. Apollodoros II.7.6.
4. Ovid *Metamorphoses* IX.101ff.
5. Sophocles *Trachiniae* 561ff.

6. Diadoros Siculus IV.36.4–7; Apollodoros II.7.6.

7. Strabo X.2.5 (trans. Loeb).

8. Apollodoros I.9.2.

9. Bakchylides *Epinic* VI.33 (Loeb).

10. Ovid *Metamorphoses* VIII, 281ff. (trans. M.M. Innes, Penguin 1955).

11. Pausanias VIII.45.5–6.

12. Homer *Iliad* IX.533.

13. Ovid *Metamorphoses* VIII.281ff.

14. Apollodoros I.8.2.

15. Apollodoros I.8.1.

16. Hesiod *Catalogue of Women and Eoiae* 14 (Loeb).

17. Apollodoros I.9.16.

18. Apollodoros I.8.2 (Loeb).

19. Aeschylus *Choephoroi* 605.

20. Apollodoros I.8.2.

21. Hyginus *Fab*.70,99 and 270; Apollodoros III.9.2; First Vatic.Mythogr. 170; Second Vatic.Mythogr. 144.

5. Other Rivers of Northwestern Greece.

1. Ovid *Metamorphoses* I.580.

2. Polybius V.110 and XXVII.16; Strabo VII.5.8.

3. Some steps have recently been cut into the side of the ravine leading down to the boulders of the stream.

6. The Peneios and Its Tributaries: Daphne's Father

1. Homer *Hymn to Apollo* 21 (Loeb).

2. Hesiod *Theogony* 343.

3. Aristotle *Historia Animalum* VI.579 (31).

4. Herodotus VII. 125–6.

5. Herodotus VII. 129 (trans. G. Rawlinson, Everyman/Dent, London 1940).

6. Pliny the Elder *Natural History* IV.8.31 (Loeb).

7. Homer *Iliad* II.748ff. (Loeb).

8. Aelian *Varia Historia* Lib.III.1; Livy XLIV.6 (Loeb).

9. John Hawkins *The Vale of Tempe*, in *Memoirs Relating to European and Asiatic Turkey* edited by Robert Walpole, XXXIV (London 1818).

10. Edward Dodwell *A Classical and Topographical Tour*, Vol. II, p.L09; London 1819.

11. Pindar *Pythian Ode* 1X (Loeb).

12. Virgil *Georgics* IV.317ff.

13. Ovid *Metamorphoses* I.567ff. (Loeb).

14. Ovid *Metamorphoses* I.452ff.

15. Pausanias X.7.8.

16. Parthenios XV.

17. Kallimachos *Iamb*. fol.5 verso, 118 (Loeb).

18. Herodotus VII. 129.

19. Strabo VIII.2.32ff. According to Nonnus (*Dionysiaca* 42.117) it was the Thessalian river god with whom Tyro fell in love. But Nonnus is a fifth-century AD epic poet. Strabo, I think, is in this instance to be preferred. Besides, according to Diadoros Siculus (IV.68), the city of Salmonis, which was founded by Tyro's father, Salmoneos, was situated on the banks of the Alpheios, near its tributary Enipios.

7. The Haliakmon, the Axios, the Strymon and the Nestos

1. Hesiod *Theogony* 341.
2. Strabo VII.
3. Homer *Iliad* II.849 (Loeb).
4. Homer *Iliad* XXI.141 (Loeb).
5. Strabo VII frag. 21 and 23.
6. Hesiod *Theogony* 338.
7. Euripides *Rhesus* 280.
8. Apollodoros I.3.4.
9. Apollodoros II.1.2 (Loeb).
10. Geryon's cattle.
11. Apollodoros. The bull had broken away.
12. Apollodoros II.5.10 (Loeb).
13. Kallimachos. *Hymn* IV to Delos 26 (Loeb).
14. Aeschylus *The Persians* 492ff. (Loeb).
15. Antiphanes in his *Thamyras* quoted by Athanaios VII.298 (Loeb).
16. Thucydides I.100.
17. Thucydides IV.104–7.
18. Herodotus VII.113–14 (trans. A. de Selincourt, Penguin 1955).
19. Herodotus VII.109.
20. Aristotle *Historia Animalum* VI.579a.31.
21. Pliny the Elder IV.40.2.
22. Pausanias VI.5.4–5 (trans. P. Levi, Penguin 1971).
23. Strabo VII.7.4; VII frag. 33.
24. Theophrastos *Enquiry into Plants* III.1.5 (Loeb).

8. The Spercheios Loved by Achilles and Its Tributaries

1. Homer *Iliad* XVI 158ff. (Loeb).
2. Scholiast on *Iliad* XXIII.142.
3. Homer *Iliad* XXIII.140ff. (Loeb).
4. Aeschylus *Choeph.* 6; Pausanias I.32.2; VIII.30.3.
5. Aeschylus *The Persians* 487 (Loeb).
6. Herodotus VII.198–9 (trans. A. de Selincourt, Penguin 1955).
7. Apollodoros II.7.7.
8. Herodotus VII.198 and Strabo II.4.14.

9. The Kephisos of Phokis and Boeotia: The Bellowing Bull

1. Homer *Hymn to Apollo* 239 (Loeb).
2. Pausanias X.35.4.
3. Homer *Iliad* II.523.
4. Pausanias X.33.2 (trans. P. Levi, Penguin 1971).
5. Ibid.
6. Pausanias X.8.5. (trans. P. Levi, Penguin 1971).

7. Ovid *Metamorphoses* III.341ff. (Loeb).
8. Hesiod *Catalogue of Women and Eoiae* 26 (Loeb).
9. The original inhabitants of Orchomenos.
10. Pausanias IX.38.6 (Loeb).

10. The Boeotian Asopos: A God of Distinguished Progeny

1. Homer *Iliad* IV.383 (Loeb).
2. Pausanias V.14.3.
3. Apollodoros III.12.6.
4. Pausanias IX.1.2.
5. Pausanias II.6.2; Homer *Odyssey* XI.260ff.
6. Pausanias II.5.2.
7. Pindar *Paean* VI.134ff.
8. D.L. Page *Corinna* (1955) and *Poetae Melia Graeci* (1962) notes 654 and 695a.
9. Pindar *Paean* VI.154ff (Loeb).

11. The Kephisos and Ilissos of Attica.

1. It appears that on the bridge the inhabitants, on their way to Eleusis, engaged in mutual jeerings of a wanton nature. See Pauly-Wissowa under *Gephyrismoi*.
2. Strabo IX.1.24 (Loeb).
3. Pausanias II.15.5.
4. Sophocles *Oedipus ad Colonus*, 668ff. (trans. R.C. Jebb, Random House 1938) .
5. Pausanias I.37.2.
6. Pausanias I.34.2.
7. Ovid *Metamorphoses* VII 670–862.
8. Apollodoros III.15.1.
9. Euripides *Ion* 1261.
10. Acropolis Museum, Room 7, No. 887.
11. National Museum of Athens, No. 1783.
12. Pausanias VIII.24.12.
13. Plato *Phaedrus* (trans. B. Jowett, Clarendon Press 1892).

Part III. The Pelopponese: Introduction

1. 'Polydiphion Argos', Homer *Iliad* IV.171.
2. Strabo VIII.6.

12. The Inachos: Punished by Poseidon

1. I have been unable to identify the Asterion, but in Argolis there are many streams that are dry throughout most of the year, one of which must have been the Asterion.
2. Pausanias II.15.5 (Loeb).
3. Pausanias II.25.3 (Loeb).
4. Apollodoros II.I.4 (Loeb).
5. Euripides *Phoinissai* 187.

6. Pausanias II.37.1 and 4.
7. Apollodoros II.1.1.
8. Hesiod *The Great Eoiae.*
9. Aeschylus *The Choephoroi* 6–7 (Loeb).
10. Aeschylus *Prometheus Bound* 589 (Loeb).
11. Ovid *Metamorphoses* I.583ff. (Loeb).

13. The Erasinos: A Vanished River God

1. Edward Dodwell *A Classical and Topographical Tour*, London 1819, Vol. II, p. 122.
2. Herodotus VI.76 (trans. G. Rawlinson, Everyman/Dent, London 1940).
3. Strabo VIII.6.8 and VIII.8.4.
4. Pausanias II.36.6.
5. Pausanias VIII.22.3. See Peter Levi's note 151 in his Penguin Classics translation of Pausanias (1971).
6. W.K. Pritchett *Studies in Ancient Topography*, Part I, p. 122.

14. The Hyllikos and the Golden Stream that Never Dies

1. Pausanias II.31.1–13 (trans. P. Levi, Penguin 1971).
2. See Peter Levi's relevant observations in his *Pausanias*, Penguin Classics, Vol. I, n. 182 p. 207 and n. 189 p. 209.

15. The Selemnos and Other Lesser Streams of the Northern Peloponnese

1. Pausanias VII.23.2 (trans. P. Levi, Penguin 1971).
2. Pausanias VII.24.4 (trans. P. Levi, Penguin 1971).
3. Homer *Iliad* II.575; VIII.203; XX.404.
4. Pausanias VII.25.6.
5. Strabo VIII.7.4.
6. Herodotus I.145.

16. The Asopos of Phleius: Sent Home with Thunderbolts

1. Akousilaos was one of the early mythographers. He lived in the fifth century BC.
2. Apollodoros III.12.6 (Loeb).
3. Statius *Thebais* VII.325ff.
4. Pausanias II.5.1–2 (Loeb).
5. Diadoros Siculus IV.72.1–5 (Loeb).
6. Apollodoros III.12.6.

17. The Styx: The Terrible Goddess

1. Hesiod *Theogony* 775ff. (Loeb).
2. Hesiod *Theogony* 361 (Loeb).

3. Pausanias VIII.17.6 (Loeb).
4. Herodotus VI.74.
5. Homer *Iliad* VIII.369; XIV.271; XV.57; *Odyssey* V.185 and 259; X.514.
6. Dante *Inferno* VII.106ff.
7. Homer *Iliad* VIII.369; *Odyssey* X.514.
8. Plato *Phaedrus* 113c.
9. Herodotus VI.74; Strabo VIII.8.4.

18. The Aroanios and Its Springs: Where the Trout Sang

1. Pausanias VIII.21.2.
2. Harry Brewster *Where the Trout Sing* (Hamish Hamilton, London 1969) p. 250.

19. The Ladon: Rich in Offspring and in Stories

1. Pausanias VIII.20.1.
2. Harry Brewster *Where the Trout Sing*, (Hamish Hamilton, London 1969) p. 250.
3. Pausanias VIII.20.1 (trans. P. Levi, Penguin 1971).
4. Pausanias VIII.20.2ff (trans. P. Levi, Penguin 1971).
5. Pausanias X.7.4.
6. Parthenios XV.
7. Ovid *Metamorphoses* I.698 (trans. M.M. Innes, Penguin 1955).
8. Nonnos *Dionysiaca* XLII.383ff. (Loeb).
9. Pausanias VIII.25.2–6.
10. Pausanias VIII.25.5 (trans. P. Levi, Penguin 1971).
11. Pausanias VIII.23.2 (trans. P. Levi, Penguin 1971).

20. The Erymanthos: Haunt of Centaurs

1. Homer *Odyssey* VI.103.
2. Pausanias VIII.24.4 (trans. P. Levi, Penguin 1971).
3. Apollodoros II.5.4; Diodoros Siculus Iv.12.3ff. Herakles is cast by Diadoros Siculus in a more favourable light than he is by Apollodoros, but the result is scarcely more flattering.
4. Pausanias VIII.24.12.

21. The Alpheios: A River God Renowned for His Lust.

1. Homer *Iliad* II.592; V.545; XI.712, 726, 728.
2. Homer *Odyssey* III.489; XV.187.
3. Homer *Hymn to Hermes*, 94ff. (Loeb).
4. Apollodoros II.5.5; Diadoros Siculus IV.13.3.
5. Diadoros Siculus IV.53.5.
6. Diadoros Siculus IV.68.1.
7. Diadoros Siculus III.66.5.
8. Pausanias 5.7.1–5 (Loeb).
9. Pindar *Nemean Ode* I (Loeb).

10. Pliny the Elder *Natural History* II.225.
11. Strabo VI.2.4 (Loeb).
12. Ovid *Metamorphoses* V.577ff. (Loeb).
13. Pausanias VI.22.9 (trans. P. Levi, Penguin 1971).
14. Pausanias V.10.7 (trans. P. Levi, Penguin 1971).
15. Strabo VIII.3.32 (Loeb).
16. Homer *Odyssey* XI.238.
17. Homer *Odyssey* XI.235ff (Loeb).
18. Apollodoros I.98.
19. Diadoros Siculus IV.68.3.
20. Lucian *Dialogues of the Gods* 13.
21. Pausanias V.7.1–2 (Loeb).
22. Pausanias VIII.28.2 (Loeb).
23. Pausanias VIII.8.8.
24. Hesiod *The Astronomy* 3.
25. Pausanias VIII.44.3 (Loeb).
26. Strabo VI.2.9 (Loeb).
27. Pausanias VIII.54.2 (Loeb).

22. The Eurotas: Ancestor of Helen

1. Pausanias VIII.4.6 (trans. P. Levi, Penguin 1971).
2. Apollodoros III.10.7.
3. Euripides *Helen* 200 (trans. E.P. Coleridge, Random House 1938).
4. Kallimachos frag. 76.
5. Pindar *Isth. Ode* I.28 (Loeb).
6. Theocritus XVIII, *The Epithalamy of Helen* 23 (Loeb).
7. Pausanias III.1.3.
8. Apollodoros I.3.3.
9. Ovid *Metamorphoses* X.161ff. (Loeb).
10. Pindar Olympic Ode VI.28.
11. Euripides *Helen.*
12. W.B. Yeats 'Leda and the Swan', *Collected Poems*, Macmillan, 1950.
13. Edward Dodwell *A Classical and Topographical Tour*, Vol. 2, p. 409.
14. Chateaubriand *Itinéraire de Paris à Jérusalem*, 1806.
15. François Pouqueville *Voyage en Maurée*, 1805 p. 86, Anne Plumtre's translation.

23. The Pamisos: A River God of Some Importance

1. Strabo VIII.4.6.
2. Pausanias IV.34.1–2 (Loeb).
3. Pausanias IV.3.10.

24. The Neda and the Lymax: Where Zeus Was Born?

1. Kallimachos Hymn I.28ff. (Loeb).
2. Apollodoros III.8.2.
3. Strabo VIII.3.22 (Loeb).
4. Pausanias IV.33.1.

5. Pausanias VIII.38.2–3.
6. H.H. Roscher *Lexikon der griechischen Mythologie*, Vol. III, p. 40 and 75f.
7. Homer *Iliad* XVIII398f.
8. Pausanias VIII.41.2–6 (Loeb).
9. Harry Brewster *Where the Trout Sing*, (Hamish Hamilton, 1969) p. 232.

INDEX

Abdera, 43

Acanameus, 41

Achaia, 57

Achaia of Phtiotis, 44, 45

Acheloös river, 2, 8, 9–14, 19, 33, 80, 81, 93; source of, 13

Acheloös, King, 9, 10, 11, 14, 22, 48, 53

Acheron river, 15–26, 30

Acherusian lake, 17

Acherusian marsh, 16, 18

Achilles, 9, 44, 45

Acrocorinth, 68

Acusilaus *see* Akousilaos

Aeacus, 67

Aegean Sea, 31

Aelian, 36, 37

Aeolus, 84

Aeschylus, 60; *The Persians*, 42

Aetios, King, 63

Agamemnon, 35

Agra, 52

Aigina, 50, 51, 67, 68

Aigion, 66

Aiolos, 81

Aitolia, 2, 4, 7, 8, 9, 10, 12, 14, 21, 23

Akarnania, 2, 7, 8, 11, 12, 17, 21

Akousilaos, 4, 67

Albania, 2

Alexander the Great, 43

Alkestis, 15

Alkmaion, 9, 13, 14

Ali Pasha, 17

Alpheios, 54, 65

Alpheios river, 2, 35, 39, 77, 80–7

Althaia, 25

Altis, 83

Amazons, 24

Ambrakia *see* Arta

Ambrakian Gulf, 13, 29

Ambrosios, 22

Amphiaraos, temple of, 53

Amphipolis, 42, 43

Amyklai, 89

Amyklas, 39, 75

Amymone, 59; river, 60

Angites stream, 43

Antiope, 50

Antiphanes, 42

Antirrhion, 22

Antony, 29

Aoös river, 27, 28, 29

Aphrodite, 26, 53, 65, 68

Apidamos, 39

Apidanus river, 34

Apollo, 21, 33, 37, 38, 39, 42, 47, 48, 66, 75, 80, 81, 89

Apollodoros, 4, 16, 22, 23, 24, 38, 41, 67, 84, 88, 89

Apollonia, 27

Arachthos river, 19, 27, 29, 30

Arcadia, 2, 58, 61, 66, 69, 70, 71, 74, 77, 80, 93, 96

Arcadians, 70, 86, 96

Archias, 81

Ares, 21

Arethusa, 65, 81, 82

Argo, 41

Argolis, 53, 57, 59, 63

Argonauts, 24

Argos, 41, 59, 60, 61
Argyra, 65
Aristaios, 5, 38
Aristotle, 33, 43
Arkas, 86
Aroanios, mount *see* Chelmos, mount
Aroanios river, 72–3
Arta, 17, 29
Artemis, 11, 23, 24, 76, 78, 81, 82, 83, 97
Artemisius, mount, 59
Asclepius, 85
Asea, 80, 86, 87
Askalaphos, 15
Asopos, 68, 76
Asopos river, Boeotian, 31, 46, 50–1
Asopos river, of Phleius, 67–8, 81
Aspripigi, 13, 33
Aspropotamos *see* Acheloös river
Asterion, 53
Asterion river, 59
Asteropaios, 9
Astraka, mount, 28
Astyoche, 16
Atalanta, 24, 25
Athenaios, 42
Athens, 43, 52
Attica, 31, 52–6
Augustus, emperor, 29
Avernus Lacus, 17
Axios river, 9, 31, 40, 41, 42

Bakhos, 10, 61
Bakchylides, 23, 68
Bassai, temple of, 96
Bellerophon, 1
Bernini, Gian Lorenzo, 38
Boebeis, lake, 34
Boeotia, 2, 4, 31, 47–9
Bolbe, 42
Bolinaios torrent, 58, 66
Boline, 66
Boreas, 42, 53, 54, 55
Boura torrent, 58, 66
Brentheates river, 85
Bulgaria, 40, 41, 43

Cadmea, 68
Calchis, 23
Centaurs, 78, 79
Chalkidike, 41
Chaon, mount, 61

Charon, 15
Chateaubriand, F.A.R., 91, 92
Chelesina, 91
Chelmos, mount, 69, 71, 72, 73, 87, 92
Chimerium, 17
Chiron, 79
Circe, 20
Cladeus river, 85
Cleitor, 70
Cleomenes, 61
Cleopatra, 25
Clitorians, 85
Colonus, 53
Corcyra, 17, 68
Corfu, 28
Corinth, 15, 27, 67; Gulf of, 2, 21
Corinthia, 57
Crete, 2, 96
Cumae, 17
Cyllene, 82
Cyphus, 35
Cyprus, 2
Cythera, 76

Damala, 63
Danaos, 59
Dante Alighieri, 17, 71
Daphne, 4, 27, 38, 39, 60, 75
Davlis, 49
Deianeira, 10, 12, 22, 23, 24, 46
Delos, 42, 81
Delphi, 9, 39, 48, 81
Demeter, 76, 77
Devil's Bridge, 63, 64
Diana, 76, 91
Dimitsana, 85
Diodoros Siculus, 4, 23, 38, 51, 68, 80, 84
Diomedes, 41
Dionysus, 53, 81
Dioskouroi, 88
Dodona, 8, 35
Dodwell, Edward, 5, 37, 61, 92, 90
Dolopia, 12, 13
Dorians, 39
Drepanon, 65
Dyras river, 45, 46

Ebasos, 41
Echeidoros river, 41
Echinades islands, 11, 12, 14, 93
Edoni, 43

Eleia, 80, 83
Elis, 39, 58, 74, 77, 81, 82, 83, 85, 96
Endymion, 4
Enianes, 45
Enienes, 35
Enipeus stream, of Elis, 84, 85
Enipeus river, 34, 39
Ephyra, 16, 17, 18
Epidauros, 41
Epirus, 2, 4, 7, 8, 13, 17, 21, 23, 27
Erasinos, 62
Erasinos river, 57, 61-2, 68
Erebos, 15
Erinys, 25
Eros, 24, 68
Erymanthos, 54
Erymanthos, mount, 79, 85
Erymanthos river, 77, 78-9, 85
Erymanthus, 82
Eryx, 41
Eteokles, 49
Euboea, 46
Euripides, 9, 41, 53; *Helen*, 88, 90; *Phoinissai*, 60
Eurotas river, 62, 81, 87, 88-92
Eurynome, 67
Eurynome, sanctuary, 97
Eurystheus, 42, 78
Eurytos, King, 46
Eustathios, 4
Evadne, 41, 89
Evenos, King, 21
Evenos river, 2, 8, 21-6, 80, 81

Frazer, James, 48, 75, 77

Gallikos river *see* Echeidoros
Gamela, mount, 27, 28
Gell, William, 5
Georgopotamos stream, 46
Getheus, 84
Glechon, 49
Glyki, 17, 18
Golden Fleece, 24
Gorgyra, 15
Gortyna, 85
Gortynios river *see* Lousios river
Gortys, 86
Gouneus, 35
Graces, 49
Gythion, 90

Hades, 15, 20, 71, 84
Haemus, mount, 41
Hago, 96
Haimos, mount, 31
Haliakmon river, 40
Haliartus, 47
Hawkins, John, 5, 36
Helen, 88, 89, 90
Helike, 66
Helikon, 1
Helisson stream, 85, 86
Helius, 68
Hephaestus, 41, 97
Hera, 42, 53, 59, 86
Heraea, 85
Herakleia of Trachis, 45, 46
Herakles, 10, 11, 12, 16, 18, 22, 23, 24, 41, 44, 46, 49, 66, 68, 78, 79, 80
Hermes, 1, 80
Hermione, 64
Herodotus, 3, 11, 12, 15, 33, 34, 39, 43, 45, 46, 61, 62, 66, 70, 71
Hesiod, 4, 9, 11, 24, 33, 41, 43, 49, 60, 69, 70, 86, 88, 97; *Theogony*, 40, 70, 80
Hiliartos, 49
Hippodameia, 83
Hippokrene spring, 1
Hippolitos, 63
Holland, Henry, 5, 17
Homer, 4, 9, 11, 15, 16, 20, 24, 25, 35, 37, 41, 50, 57, 66, 70, 71, 78, 80, 84, 88, 97; *Iliad*, 2, 41, 45, 47, 80, 97; *Odyssey*, 80
Horace, 91
Hughes, Thomas, 5
Hyakinthos, 4, 89
Hydra, 23, 60
Hyginus, 4
Hyllikos river, 3, 57, 63-4
Hypseos, 38

Iasos, 25
Ida, mount (Crete), 1
Ida, mount (Mysia), 1
Idas, 21
Igoumenitsa, 28
Ilissos river, 31, 52-6
Illyria, 27
Inachos, king, 96
Inachos river, 3, 13, 52, 57, 59-60, 86
Io, 60
Ioannina, 27, 28, 29; lake, 62

Iole, 46
Ionian Sea, 2, 7, 28, 42, 80
Iris, 69, 71
Ismenas, 67
Ithome, mount, 93

Kalavrita, 77
Kallimachos, 39, 42
Kallirhoe, 14
Kallisto, 76, 86
Kalydon, 23, 24, 25, 26
Karditsa, 13
Karitena, 86
Kastalia, 48; spring, 9
Kastalian spring, 39
Kastor, 88
Kephalari spring, 61, 62
Kephalos, 53, 54
Kephisos river, 48, 59
Kephisos river, of Attica, 2, 31, 52–6
Kephisos river, of Boeotia, 47–9
Kerausion, mount, 96
Keseriani monastery, 54
Kithairon, mount, 1, 50
Kladeos, stream, 54, 83
Kleomenes, 70
Klytaimnestra, 88
Kokytos river, 17, 18, 20
Konitsa, 28
Kopai, 49
Korax, mount, 21
Korinna, 50
Kotilion, mount, 95
Koutailares, island, 14
Krathis river, 58, 66, 70
Krathis stream, 58, 69
Kriasos, 41
Kreusa, 38
Kuretes, 25
Kyllene mount, 1, 68
Kyrene, 38

Laconia, 87
Laconian gulf, 90
Ladon, 38, 75
Ladon river, 2, 67, 74–7, 81, 85
Lakedaimon, King, 88, 89
Lakmon, mount, 13, 33
Lakonia, 58, 91, 92
Lampeia, mount, 78
Lapiths, 1, 78

Laryma, 49
Leake, William, 5, 18, 49
Lear, Edward, 5
Leda, 4, 88, 90, 92
Leleges, 88
Lelex, 88
Lerna, 59, 60
Lernian springs, 60
Lestenitsa stream, 39, 84
Leto, 76
Letrini, 83
Leucas, 17
Leukippos, 75
Lilaia, 47, 48
Liriope, 48
Livy, 27, 29, 35, 36, 37
Lougaras, 87
Louros river, 29
Lousios river, 29, 35, 85, 86
Lucian, 84
Lycaeus, mount, 76
Lyceium, 52
Lycormas, river, 23
Lykaion, 95
Lykaion, mount, 83, 95, 96
Lykormas river, 21
Lymax river, 3, 29, 85, 95–8

Maeander river, 93
Maenalus, 82
Magalopolis, 87
Magnesia, 42
Maina hills, 90
Mainalon, mount, 1, 86
Makedonia, 2, 3, 31, 33, 40, 41, 42, 43
Malian gulf, 45
Malis, 44, 45
Margarition, 20
Marpessa, 21
Mavroneri see Styx river
Megalopolis, 85, 86, 87
Melaeneae, 85
Melanion, 26
Meleager, 24, 25
Menesthius, 44
Mercury, 76
Merope, 76
Mesolonghi, 22
Messenia, 58, 93, 94, 96
Meteora, 34
Methana, 63

Michelangelo, 90
Migdovas *see* Tauropos river
Miles, 88
Minyans, 49
Mistra, 91
Muses, 1, 9, 53
Mycenae, 60
Mysia, 40

Naiads, 2, 13, 47, 97
Narkissos, 48, 49
Neaera, 41
Neda, 95
Neda river, 2, 29, 85, 95–8
Nekyomanteion, 15, 18
Nemea, 68
Nereids, 97
Nessos, 22, 23, 46, 79
Nessus river *see* Nestos
Nestos river, 33, 40, 43
Nikopolis, 29
Nile river, 11, 80
Nine Ways, 42, 43
Nonacris, 70
Nonnos, 76
Nykteos, 50

Ocalea, 47
Ocean, 16
Oceanus river, 20
Odysseos, 16, 20, 84
Oedipos, 53
Oeneos, King, 10, 12, 23
Oeniadai, 10, 12, 14
Oenoë, 59
Oenomaos, 21
Oenome, 4
Oenone, 67, 68
Oeta, mount, 44, 45
Oinomaos, 75
Okeanos, 2, 9, 33, 40, 50, 60, 67, 69, 70, 80, 97
Oltos, 11
Olympia, 39, 54, 80, 82, 83
Olympus, mount, 1, 2, 34, 36, 40, 69, 71, 91
Onochonos river, 34, 39
Ophians, 23
Orchomenos, 49, 82
Orcus river, 35
Oreithyia, 53, 54
Orestes, 60
Oropos, 50

Ortygia, 81, 83
Ossa, mount, 1, 34, 36
Othrys, mount, 34, 39, 46
Ovid, 4, 11, 22, 23, 24, 27, 39, 48, 53, 60, 75, 76, 82, 83; *Metamorphoses*, 5, 10, 38, 75, 89
Oxeia, island, 14

Palla, 70
Pallas Athena, 16
Pamisus river, 34, 93–4
Pan, 1, 61, 64, 75, 76, 78, 86
Panachaikon, mount, 66
Pangaion, mount, 42, 43
Panopeos, 49
Panyanis, 48
Paracheloitis, 12
Paramythia, 17, 20
Paris, 1
Parnassos, mount, 1, 46, 47, 48
Parnes, mount, 50, 53
Parthenios, 39, 75
Parthenon, 53, 54
Parthenopaios, 25
Patras, 65
Patroklos, 45
Pausanias, 3, 4, 5, 16, 20, 24, 39, 43, 48, 49, 51, 53, 54, 59, 60, 61, 62, 63, 64, 65, 66, 67, 68, 70, 72, 74, 75, 76, 77, 78, 79, 81, 83, 85, 86, 88, 89, 93, 94, 96, 97
Pegai, 72, 87
Pegasos, 1
Peirene, 68
Pelagon, 41, 67
Peleos, 24, 44, 45
Pelion, mount, 1, 34, 38, 46, 78
Peloponnese, 2, 3, 41, 74, 75, 93
Peloponnesian War, 43
Pelops, 83
Peneios river, 2, 31, 33–9, 40, 60
Pentelikon, mount, 53
Peraebi, 35
Periander, 15
Periboea, 41
Periphlegeton river, 16
Peristeri, 13
Pero, 67
Persephone, 15, 18, 20, 25
Phaidra, 63
Phaidros, 55
Phaleric Gulf, 52
Phea, 95

Phenean lake, 75
Pheneus, 70
Phigalia, 96, 97
Phigalians, 85
Philip II, 43
Philyra, 95
Phleius, 68
Phokis, 47–9, 68
Phokos, 68
Pholoe, mount, 78, 79
Pholos, 79
Phoroneus, 59
Phryxios river, 62
Phtios, 45
Phtiotis, 44, 45, 46
Phylas, 16
Phyllis, 43
Pindar, 9, 38, 49, 50, 68, 81
Pindos range, 2, 4, 7, 8, 12, 13, 27, 29, 31, 33, 34, 38, 46
Piras, 41
Pitane, 89
Pitani, 91
Plataia, 50; battle of, 50
Plato, 16, 71, 91
Plato, *Phaidros*, 52, 54, 55
Pleuron, 23
Pliny, 35, 36, 37, 43, 81
Pollaiuolo, A. del, 38
Pollux, 88, 89, 90
Polybius, 27, 29
Polycaon, 88
Polydora, 44
Poseidon, 21, 34, 53, 59, 60, 66, 67, 76, 77, 84, 85, 89
Pouqueville, François, 5, 91, 92
Prokris, 53, 54
Prometheus, 60
Psophis, 54, 79, 82
Puteoli, 17
Pyriphlegeton river, 20

Rhea, 98
Rhesos, 41
Rhodope, mount, 31

Salmoneos, 39, 80, 84
Salmonia, 81
Saronic gulf, 63
Scheria, 68
Schonoeneus, 24

Selemnos stream, 58, 65
Selinos stream, 58, 66
Sicily, 2, 82
Sikyon, 68
Sikyonians, 50, 51
Sirens, 9, 97
Sisyphos, 67, 68
Skamander river, 2, 40
Skopas, 24
Smolikas, mount, 27
Socrates, 54, 55
Solos village, 70
Sophocles, 10, 16, 53; *Trachiniae*, 10, 22, 46
Souli: fortresses, 19; range, 18; Seraglio of, 17
Sparta, 39, 70, 88, 89, 90, 91, 92
Spartans, 43, 45
Spercheios, 44
Spercheios river, 2, 31, 44–6
Stageira, 33
Statius, 67
Stomion, 97
Strabo, 3, 4, 5, 12, 13, 23, 27, 28, 29, 34, 39, 40, 41, 52, 53, 57, 61, 62, 71, 81, 82, 84, 87, 93, 96
Stratos, 12, 14
Struma, 41
Strymon river, 31, 40, 41, 42, 43
Stymphalian lake, 61, 68
Stymphalian wood, 82
Stymphalos, 62
Styx river, 16, 20, 35, 66, 69–71, 95
Syracuse, 81
Syrinx, 4, 75, 76

Takka, lake, 62, 87
Tanagra, 50
Tartaros, 17
Tauropos river, 13
Taygetos range, 93
Tegea, temple of, 24
Tegean plain, 87
Tempe, Vale of, 5, 34, 35, 36, 37, 38
Tethys, 2, 9, 33, 40, 50, 60, 67, 80
Teztzes, 4
Thamyris, 89
Thaumas, 69
Thebans, 49, 50
Thebe, 10, 50, 68
Theisoa, 96
Thelpousa, 76, 78
Theophrastos, 43
Thermaic Gulf, 41

Thermopylai, 46
Theseus, 10, 11, 16, 63
Thesprotia, 15, 16, 17, 18, 20
Thessalonika, 41
Thessaly, 2, 8, 33, 34, 40, 44, 46
Thestios, 25
Thetis, 97
Thrace, 3, 41, 42, 43
Thucydides, 12, 13, 17, 27, 28, 43
Thyamis river, 28, 62
Titaressos river, 35, 40
Tomaros, mount, 8, 29
Trachian mountains, 44, 45, 47
Trachis, 46
Tragos river, 77
Trinemeis, 52
Tripolis, 77, 87
Tripotamos, 78, 79
Trizenia, 64
Troizen, 63
Troy, 1, 41

Tymphe, mount, 8, 28, 29
Tymphrestos, mount, 44, 46
Tyndareos, 88, 89
Tyro, 39, 84

Viko gorge, 27, 28
Vinci, Leonardo da, 90
Virgil, 4, 5, 17, 38, 76
Voidomati river, 27, 28

Xerxes, 33, 39, 41, 42, 43

Yeats, W.B., 90
Yugoslavia, 40, 41

Zagoria region, 7
Zagouri, stream, 17
Zeus, 9, 10, 16, 26, 44, 51, 60, 63, 67, 69, 83, 85,
    86, 88, 90, 95, 96, 98
Zeus Saviour, 64
Zoumerka, mount, 13, 29